FINDING GOD
IN THE
HOBBIT

FINDING GOD
IN
H(THE)OBBIT

JIM WARE

SALT**RIVER**®

AN IMPRINT OF TYNDALE HOUSE PUBLISHERS, INC.

Visit Tyndale's exciting Web site at www.tyndale.com

TYNDALE is a registered trademark of Tyndale House Publishers, Inc.

SaltRiver and the SaltRiver logo are registered trademarks of Tyndale House Publishers, Inc.

The Hobbit is a trademark of the Saul Zaentz Company dba Tolkien Enterprises.

Finding God in The Hobbit

Designed by Luke Daab

Published in association with the literary agency of Alive Communications, Inc., 7680 Goddard Street, Suite 200, Colorado Springs, CO 80920.

Scripture taken from the New King James Version. Copyright © 1979, 1980, 1982 by Thomas Nelson, Inc. Used by permission. All rights reserved.

Library of Congress Cataloging-in-Publication Data

Ware, Jim
    Finding God in The Hobbit / Jim Ware.
        p. cm.
    Includes bibliographical references.
    ISBN-13: 978-1-4143-0596-7
    ISBN-10: 1-4143-0596-6
    1. Tolkien, J. R. R. (John Ronald Reuel), 1892-1973. Hobbit. 2. Tolkien, J. R. R. (John Ronald Reuel), 1892-1973—Religion. 3. Fantasy fiction, English—History and criticism.
4. Christianity in literature. 5. Religion in literature. 6. Baggins, Bilbo (Fictitious character)
7. Hobbits (Fictitious characters) 8. Middle Earth (Imaginary place) I. Title.
    PR6039.O32H638 2006
    823'.912—dc22   2006012339

Printed in the United States of America

11   10   09   08   07   06
7   6   5   4   3   2   1

Dedication

In memory of my dad,
a wise counselor in the journey of life

Table of Contents

Foreword

by Kurt Bruner

No child should grow up in a world without hobbits. Trust me; I'm one who was raised in a home that did not contain a single copy of the book. So I didn't become acquainted with Bilbo, Gandalf, or their dwarf companions until well into my adult years. In fact, I had children of my own before reading the famous hobbit's "there and back again" adventure. Knowing what it is to endure such a deprived youth, I want something better for my kids. That's why I've included J. R. R. Tolkien's *The Hobbit* on their list of mandatory delights.

No self-respecting list of recommended children's literature would leave off Tolkien's classic tale, a story that introduced the world to Middle-earth, magic rings, and nasty orcs. Its pages show children (and adults like me) just how much a reluctant hero can achieve when forced out of his "hole in the ground" comfort zone. And somewhere along the journey, the story manages to inspire our hearts with realities best experienced in the land of fantasy.

J. R. R. Tolkien added words like *Baggins* and *Balrog* to our vocabulary through his imaginative art. But he also added concepts that grow out of deep commitment to Christian orthodoxy. Most notably, he showed us what it means to create another world—or more properly, sub-create it. You see, Professor Tolkien did not refer to his writing as an act of creation. He called it an act of "sub-creation." As a devout Christian, he believed that there is one Creator and that men and women made in the image of that Creator have the capacity and calling to participate in God's ongoing work. But we do so humbly in the spirit of Psalm 45:1: "My tongue is the pen of a skillful writer." The pen can take no pride in what ends up on the page. Rather, it is honored to have played any part at all in the composition. Tolkien called ours the "primary world" spoken into existence by the primary artist. All other creativity, including fantasy literature, is a mere reflection of ultimate reality. He gave birth to Middle-earth as he fathered his children, by becoming a tool in the hand of the true author of life. He built his world like a carpenter builds a table, fashioning wood received from the ground.

A delightful element in Tolkien's unique creation grew out of his passion for words. As a philologist, he loved the texture and composition of spoken and written language. In fact, he invented several of his own—including the haunting elvish script that famously appears on the ring of doom. Other writers might have hastily thrown together symbols and scribbles to suggest another dialect. But Tolkien went much further, painstakingly crafting an entire alphabet and glossary possessing an internal consistency that rivals any modern language. I'll never forget the first time I received a "Happy Birthday" note from a coworker written in the elvish tongue. It was then that I realized some people take J. R. R. Tolkien very seriously.

As well they should. *World* magazine ranked Tolkien's writings among the greatest works of Christian imagination ever penned. Many found such ranking a surprise because, unlike John Bunyan's *The Pilgrim's Progress* or other works of allegory, *The Hobbit* and *The Lord of the Rings* contain no reference to God and seem stained with the influence of a foreboding evil hardly consistent with the good news of the gospel. What many miss, however, is how foundational foreboding evil is to Tolkien's theology and creativity. Which brings me to another concept and word he added to my vocabulary—*eucatastrophe*.

I first encountered the word while reading Professor Tolkien's essay entitled "On Fairy-Stories," in which he describes his philosophy of story-telling. It caused me pause. I knew that the word *catastrophe* meant something tragic spoiling an otherwise happy life, such as a tornado destroying one's home or cancer invading one's body. But what, pray tell, did he mean by *eucatastrophe*?

In order to explain, I need you to think about a closing scene in *The Sound of Music*. Do you remember the moment when Nazis pursuing the von Trapp family find it impossible to start their cars outside the abbey even as two nuns confess to the Reverend Mother their sin of stealing engine parts? Their unexpected action saves the day—so we laugh, both at the humor of the moment and the relieved assurance that our heroes will indeed escape. The surprise of both prompts a deeply satisfying laughter, a laughter made possible by the prior tension of evil Nazis and seemingly imminent doom. That scene is a small taste of "eucatastrophe." Rather than an invasion of sorrow, it is the surprise of joy bursting onto a seemingly hopeless situation; the certainty of death and destruction undone by the unexpected intrusion of life and resurrection. In a word, the gospel.

The gospel permeates Middle-earth not because of any overt reference to God, redemption, or the four spiritual laws. The gospel permeates Middle-earth because, as Jim Ware so ably demonstrates, the surprise of joy invades at the most unexpected moments—prompting the only appropriate response, laughter. We chuckle at the irony of a reluctant adventurer named Baggins joining a rough-and-ready group of much larger dwarves in search of fortune. We laugh when giant trolls eager to eat a trembling Bilbo instead argue themselves into stone. We giggle as the tiny, awkward hobbit rescues his captured companions by sending them downriver in cramped, spinning barrels. And through it all, we delight in the experience of an author who sub-created a world that echoes primary reality where good overtakes evil, light dispels darkness, and the surprise of joy invades a story of woe.

I know you will enjoy these reflections on *The Hobbit* offered by my friend and coauthor Jim Ware. Like earlier books in our Finding God series, its chapters surface tasty morsels of spiritual nourishment buried deep within the writings of a skillful artist. Don't be surprised to encounter God in unexpected places. After all, that's what the gospel is all about.

Introduction

On a frosty evening in October 1916, just as the light was fading from the sky and the hills above the Dorking valley were melting into shadow and mist, a young man stepped up to the bookstall at the Leatherhead rail station in Surrey, England. Squinting into the gathering dusk, he saw the train rumbling up the track under a cloud of black smoke undershot with a tinge of red firelight. He'd just have time to pick up something for the ride home and a bit of weekend reading. Hastily he selected a slim volume in a soiled paper jacket, pulled a few shillings from his pocket, and laid them on the counter.

Neither the bookseller, who totted up the money without so much as an upward glance, nor the porter, who stood blowing on mittened hands at the other end of the platform, had the slightest idea that a historic event had just taken place. Yet so it was; for the purchase of that little book proved to be a spiritual turning point, not only for the buyer, but for the millions who have since felt the impact of his life, his thought, and his voluminous literary work.

The young man was C. S. Lewis—"Jack" to his friends—one of the most popular and effective Christian apologists of the last century, author of such perennial classics as The Chronicles of Narnia, *Perelandra, Mere Christianity, The Problem of Pain,* and *The Screwtape Letters.* The book was George MacDonald's *Phantastes.*

What was it that made Jack's purchase of this relatively obscure nineteenth-century "faerie romance" such a momentous transaction? Why in later life did he look back upon it as a watershed experience—a vital passage in his journey from atheism to Christian devotion, a crucial step in his personal quest for joy? *Phantastes* was, after all, just another "fairy tale," a story similar in many respects to scores of others he'd been imbibing since childhood: the heroic fantasies of William Morris and Lord Dunsany, for example, or the Arthurian legends of Sir Thomas Malory, or the myths of the Norsemen. What made this tale different?

Jack explains:

> In one sense the new country was exactly like the old. I met there all that had already charmed me in Malory, Spenser, Morris, and Yeats. But in another sense all was changed. I did not yet know (and I was long in learning) the name of the new quality, the bright shadow, that rested on the travels of Anodos. I do now. It was Holiness.[1]

He concludes with these remarkable words:

That night my imagination was, in a certain sense,
baptised; the rest of me, not unnaturally, took longer.
I had not the faintest notion what I had let myself in
for by buying *Phantastes*.[2]

"Sanity and Sanctity"

Lewis must have been about seventeen when he stumbled
onto George MacDonald on the platform at Leatherhead
station. I was about the same age—a year or two younger,
perhaps—when I met J. R. R. Tolkien. I don't mean literally, of course. Though Tolkien was still living at the time,
I never did manage to make the long trip from Van Nuys,
California, to Poole, England, in order to shake his hand. Instead, I got acquainted with him in the same way Lewis got
acquainted with MacDonald—through one of his books. In
my case, the book was *The Hobbit*.

Unlike Lewis, I don't have a dramatic Christian conver-
sion story to tell in conjunction with my reading of *The
Hobbit*. I was already a believer (albeit a very *young* believer)
when the book came into my hands, so I never felt compelled
to credit Tolkien with baptizing my imagination or any
other part of my spiritual or psychological anatomy. But I *can*

affirm that his writing has had a profound impact on my life nonetheless.

I suppose the simplest way of explaining this is to say that I made a discovery during the course of my travels with Bilbo Baggins, a discovery that closely parallels the one Jack Lewis made in the land of *Phantastes*. In *The Hobbit* I was swept up into a story that was at once completely familiar to me (I was a confirmed fan of legend, myth, and fairy tale) and yet at the same time delightfully strange and new. In the beginning I sensed this difference mainly in terms of *atmosphere*: an air of goodness, health, rightness, purity, and truth—something like the "holiness" Jack found in his wanderings with Anodos. Most fifteen-year-old boys don't spend much time thinking about this sort of thing. But they are fully capable of *feeling* it. And feel it I did, to my great benefit and everlasting gain.

Apparently I'm not the only one who has ever had this impression of the imaginary world of Middle-earth. In the autumn of 1971, Miss Carole Batten-Phelps wrote a letter to Tolkien in which she spoke of finding "a sanity and sanctity" in his tales that she considered "a power in itself." Deeply moved, the author of *The Hobbit* and *The Lord of the Rings* responded by saying that he had just received *another* letter from *another* reader containing a remarkably similar comment. After characterizing himself as "an unbeliever, or at best a man of belatedly and dimly dawning religious feeling," the writer of this other letter had gone on to declare: "But you . . . create a world in which some sort of faith seems to be everywhere without a visible source, like light from an invisible lamp."[3]

I am here to say that I have tasted that "sanity and sanctity." At a critical point in my life, I stood within the circle of light cast by that "invisible lamp." I now believe that *The Hobbit* was part of a constellation of diverse influences that came together to prepare me for a deeper and truer experience of divine grace—an experience that, strangely enough, began to blossom within a matter of months after my initial encounter with Tolkien and Bilbo Baggins. As you can imagine, this is one of my most cherished personal memories, for reasons I'll explain in greater detail in the final pages of this book. But that experience is something more as well: It is also the chief reason I find so much joy in the prospect of leading others on a quest to find God in the pages of *The Hobbit*.

Intentions and Beliefs

Where there is light, there must be a light source, invisible and concealed though it may be. Whence comes the pervasive illumination that Miss Batten-Phelps and I and that other "man of belatedly and dimly dawning religious feeling" have perceived in the works of J. R. R. Tolkien?

One thing is certain: It does not proceed from what we might call "calculated religiosity." Tolkien was *not* on a campaign to convert the masses by writing cleverly disguised evangelistic tracts. In his introduction to our book *Finding God in The Lord of the Rings*, my writing partner Kurt Bruner states, "*The Lord of the Rings* is not, as some have suggested, a covert allegory of the gospel. . . . Tolkien was telling a story, not proclaiming a message."[4]

I want to revisit this idea of allegory once we've come to the end of our tour of Mr. Baggins's journey through the wild. For now it's enough to note that what Kurt says is absolutely true. And there is probably no book of which it is truer than *The Hobbit*, a tale that seems to have sprung to life of its own accord when, for reasons he himself couldn't explain, the author picked up a pen and scrawled ten little words—"In a hole in the ground there lived a hobbit"—on the blank page of a student examination booklet.

But while Tolkien didn't set out to teach lessons or preach sermons, few will deny that his stories are rich in spiritual significance and filled with images of transcendent truth. There's a good reason for this. At a certain level, an artist's character and worldview are more important than his stated goals and intentions; as the wise man observes, "As he thinks in his heart, so is he" (Proverbs 23:7), and this inevitably comes through in his work. To put it another way, the proof is in the pudding. And the writer's most deeply held beliefs and convictions are generally in his tale.

INTRODUCTION

"The Purpose of Life"

What exactly were Tolkien's convictions and beliefs? Some of his fans might be surprised to discover how straight-forward he was on this point. "I am a Christian," he declares in a 1958 letter to Deborah Webster, adding that, in his view, this fact "can be deduced from my stories."[5] Elsewhere he explains that while he felt under no obligation to make his imaginary world fit in with formalized theology, "I actually intended it to be consonant with Christian thought and belief."[6]

In another place, he says that "one object" of his "sub-creative" endeavors was "the elucidation of truth, and the encouragement of good morals in this real world, by the ancient device of exemplifying them in unfamiliar embodiments, that may tend to 'bring them home'"[7]—a statement that bears a striking resemblance to C. S. Lewis's musings on the theme of "steal[ing] past . . . watchful dragons" and "casting" Christian truths "into an imaginary world, stripping them of their stained-glass and Sunday school associations, [so that] one could make them for the first time appear in their real potency."[8]

But perhaps the most touching and impressive of Tolkien's many written professions of his personal faith is to be found in a letter he penned to young Camilla Unwin in May 1969, when the author was seventy-seven years of age.

As part of a school project, Camilla had been assigned to write to a well-known person and pose the question: "What is the purpose of life?"

Tolkien responded:

> If you do not believe in a personal God, the question: 'What is the purpose of life?' is unaskable and unanswerable.
>
> . . . It may be said that the chief purpose of life, for any one of us, is to increase according to our capacity our knowledge of God by all the means we have, and to be moved by it to praise and thanks. To do as we say in the *Gloria in Excelsis*: . . . We praise you, we call you holy, we worship you, we proclaim your glory, we thank you for the greatness of your splendor.[9]

Praise and thanks. Worship and splendor. Greatness and glory and holiness. I will testify to having found all this and more in the story of Mr. Bilbo Baggins, Esquire, the unlikely adventurer from Bag-End in the Shire.

"How so?" you ask.

"Ah!" I respond. "If you really want to know, read on. . . ."

A Personal Note

"No real lover of Tolkien's fiction," writes Clyde Kilby, "would want it turned into sermons, no matter how cleverly preached."[10] In our study of *The Lord of the Rings*, Kurt Bruner and I make it clear that we mean to stay true to the spirit of Kilby's pronouncement. Similarly, in the foreword to our book of reflections on C. S. Lewis's Narnia tales (*Finding God in the Land of Narnia*), we state that it is not our intention "to turn Lewis's stories into sermons."[11]

It's only fair to tell you, however, that in the present volume all bets are off. If I feel like preaching a sermon, I might just go ahead and do it (in which case you should bear in mind that *sermon* isn't a dirty word; in Latin, *sermo* means nothing more than "conversation" or "friendly talk"). If I want to stretch a point or turn a scene from *The Hobbit* into a springboard to something else, something that seems unrelated to the tale, I may indulge myself in this regard as well (in which case I apologize in advance). That's because this book is designed to be about something more than J. R. R. Tolkien, Bilbo Baggins, and the ins and outs of Middle-earth. To a certain degree, it's also meant to be a book about *me*: my life, my thoughts, and my feelings about God and the world and Christian spirituality.

My hope, of course, is that to the extent it succeeds in being a book about *me*, it will also turn out to be a book about *you*—a book with which you can connect on a personal, heartfelt level. We are, after all, members of the same human family: men and women who know the same longings, groan under the same burdens, and exult in the same simple joys—brothers and sisters made in the likeness of the Father and Creator of us all.

In any case, you've been properly warned.

A DREAM
COME TRUE?

Snuggled down beneath the bedclothes, staring sleepless into the darkness, Bilbo put forth one last effort to make sense of the absurd events of the past six hours.

"Dwarves!" he fumed. "Dwarvish racket! Dwarvish talk of journeys and dragons and treasures and burglaries! Dwarves on the doorstep and dwarves in the parlor! Dwarves demanding seed-cakes and raspberry tarts with their tea—not to mention my best ale!" He snorted in disgust. What would his father, the respectable Bungo Baggins, have said? "It's a wonder the pantry wasn't left completely bare!"

"Ah! But then you've been known to hobnob with dwarves before this," cautioned a voice from the other side of his

I

brain—a voice suspiciously reminiscent of his grandfather, the scandalous Old Took. "In fact, you've acquired something of a reputation for associating with outlandish folk of all sorts. It's rumored you've even been seen with elves."

"That's beside the point," protested the practical Baggins part of him. "It was thoughtless of Gandalf. Not that I want to appear inhospitable. But an uninvited crowd at tea-time is quite enough to push any hobbit beyond his limits!"

"Limits?" The Took side of him laughed softly. "What do you know of limits? How will you *ever* know if you don't step outside the door and leave your pantry behind?"

A breath of wind caught the curtains. Outside the crickets had raised a chorus in the hedge. Was it really a hint of elvish music that Bilbo heard wafting on the breeze? A scent of spring and wakening earth and approaching summer stirred a nameless longing deep within him; and the Took side, seeing its chance, stung him with an unforgiving pang of wanderlust. Bilbo sighed and turned his face to the wall.

"You're right, of course," he muttered miserably. "It's what I've always wanted! But in middle age a hobbit realizes that some dreams just have to remain private."

"Private or not," the Took side said, "I have a feeling that *your* dream is about to come true."

Out in the parlor the dwarves had taken up their song again:

A DREAM COME TRUE?

Far over the misty mountains cold
To dungeons deep and caverns old
We must away, ere break of day,
To find our long-forgotten gold.

Bilbo moaned and drew the covers up over his head.

* * * * *

To sleep! Perchance to dream . . .

Ay, there's the rub indeed. For dreams can shatter restful, comfortable slumber. And the ramifications of a dream come true aren't always what you had expected. Hopes and longings nurtured in the secret darkness have a way of taking on a very different shape in the daylight of reality.

Once there was a man who had a dream. For thirty-eight years he lay stretched on a miserable mat beside a miraculous pool, lame, unable to rise, waiting for an angel to stir the water, cherishing a vision of himself leaping and skipping like a boy. It was a vision that seemed unlikely to be realized. But it kept him alive, and he clung to it as a child clings to an empty bottle or a scrap of an old blanket.

Then one day it happened. The dream emerged from the shadows and greeted him with a thumping, hearty "Hello!" It took him by the hand and searched his face with dark, piercing eyes. Then it said, "Do you want to be made well?"

And, strange as it seems, he found that he *could not* respond with a simple yes (see John 5:1-8).

This is one of the great paradoxes of the human condition: the debilitating fear that so often raises its head when the thing you've always wanted is suddenly presented to you on a silver platter. When a prospective employer calls back to say, "You're hired," or the girl of your dreams accepts your proposal. Even the boldest among us knows what it is like to shrink before the incarnation of our own most deeply held desires. It's an odd but extremely common experience.

Bilbo Baggins, the furry-footed, middle-aged, comfortably situated hero of J. R. R. Tolkien's classic tale *The Hobbit*, ran up against this paradox when *his* dream came knocking at the door one afternoon in late April. Bilbo, it seems, was not like other hobbits. Most of *them* were content to stay at home in front of the fire with a foaming pint or a cup of tea. *He*, on the other hand, was subject to chronic fits of restlessness and discontent. Not that he was unappreciative of his creature comforts—he was, after all, the son of a Baggins. Still, there was something in his makeup, something rooted in the unpredictable eccentricities of his maternal kin, the Tooks, that inclined him to pine for journeys and adventures and woodland trysts with elves.

How odd, then, that on this night of nights he should find himself lying in his bed, trembling at the sound of his dream coming true on the other side of the wall. His unexpected

visitors, the dwarves, were singing again. It was the same al-
luring, spellbinding song that had stirred him so profoundly
earlier in the evening: the one about enchanted gold and caverns old and the dangers of the long and winding road. This
was just the sort of thing he'd been waiting for all his life.
Why, then, this fluttering and churning in his stomach? this
feeling that he wanted them all to go away and leave him
alone?

Gandalf knew exactly what the hobbit was feeling—and
why:

> Bilbo had changed, of course. At least, he was getting
> rather greedy and fat, and his old desires had dwin-
> dled down to a sort of private dream. Nothing could
> have been more dismaying than to find it actually in
> danger of coming true![12]

A private dream is a sweet and succulent thing. It's like an
obscure hobby or an old romantic movie or a book in a cozy
corner on a rainy afternoon. It's a source of solace in the
midst of life's disappointments; a place of retreat far from
the madding crowd, where the world becomes whatever one
wants it to be. But a dream come true is another matter alto-
gether. For in the final analysis, a dream come true is nothing
but a call to commitment and *action*.

I understand what Bilbo was up against. I experienced it
myself when I got my first chance to write a book for

publication—something I'd been wanting to do since child-hood. Somehow the unforeseen opportunity set off alarm bells inside my head. Instantly all the dreadful implications of actual authorship stood ranged before me like a troop of treasure-hunting dwarves: the hard work, the battle with discouragement, the potential for criticism, the possibility of failure. I was seized with an irrational desire to scream, "You don't understand—I was only kidding!" Like Bilbo, I wished that it would all go away and leave me alone.

Similarly, while our personal dreams are as individual as our fingerprints, each of us was created with a longing, a dream if you will, for fellowship with our Maker. While the "Baggins" in us may be satisfied to putter along without the challenge of His mystery, power, and love, the "Took" knows very well that it was created for bigger things. And so in private moments and secret places, like Nicodemus, the clandestine disciple who sought Christ only under cover of darkness (John 3:2), we grope after Him with unutterable groanings and inconsolable longings. Like the psalmist we cry, "My soul longs, yes, even faints for the courts of the LORD; my heart and my flesh cry out for the living God" (Psalm 84:2). Then, when He shows up on the doormat and says, "Come out into the light and follow Me!" we retreat to a back bedroom, hoping He'll leave if we pretend nobody's at home. Like Moses we whine, "O Lord, you've got the wrong person! Please send somebody else!" (See Exodus 4:13.)

A DREAM COME TRUE?

Jesus Christ *is* our dream come true. He is the Desire of All Nations—and the Desire of All Nations *has* come. The problem is that we find the tonic of the adventure He offers too bracing for our tame sensibilities and tastes. He is not the kind of Savior we were expecting. He shatters our repose with shocking statements about dividing swords, the joys of suffering, and the rejection of the Son of Man. He frightens us with bizarre and uncompromising demands. Leave home and family. Sell what you have and give to the poor. Allow yourself to be hated and persecuted for My sake. Take up your cross and follow Me.

What does it all mean? If *this* is what the journey holds for those who answer the Master's call, who can expect to be saved?

Like Bilbo, we will never know until we throw off the covers, jump out of bed, and somehow find the courage to step up on the road.

REFLECTION
Be sure your dream will find you out!

As they sang the hobbit felt the love of beautiful things made by hands and by cunning . . . the desire of the hearts of dwarves.

—THE HOBBIT, CHAPTER I, "AN UNEXPECTED PARTY"

THINGS BRIGHT AND BEAUTIFUL

It was not until the following morning that Bilbo, running down the road to Bywater without hat, money, or even a pocket-handkerchief, had a moment to ask himself what it was about these dwarves and their quest that had so deeply touched his Tookish side. Why, as recently as ten minutes ago, had he made the rash decision to accept their offer and join them at the Green Dragon Inn?

It certainly wasn't the way they asked, he reflected. *Manners are not their strong suit. Thorin is a bit imperious if you ask me. As for the rest of them, I'm not sure they want my services at all. More like a grocer than a burglar indeed!*

Yet here he was, panting and puffing, hurrying to keep his

appointment with the treasure seekers—and with his own destiny. It wasn't until he rounded a corner and came within sight of the inn that the reason for his inexplicable behavior suddenly dawned upon him.

There above the door, swaying slightly in the cool morning breeze, hung the proprietor's signboard: a square placard carved and painted with the figure of a rampant dragon, bright green and glittering with gilded scales. So deft was the workmanship that the serpent's lithe body seemed to emerge from the wood, flowing and rippling with the gentle motion of the air. Its great webbed, batlike wings flashed red in the sunlight.

In that instant it all came back to him. Again he heard the dwarves' song of the dragon-hoard. Again he saw the light in their eyes when they spoke of valuable family heirlooms and the making of fine, handcrafted things. All of this moved him deeply, for Bilbo was no stranger to the love of beauty. He had, in fact, filled Bag-End with all sorts of lovely items that brought him no end of pleasure: porcelain trinkets, rare paintings, silver utensils, china teacups. He was no dwarf, but he could easily understand the affection of dwarves for all that was skillfully wrought and fair.

Funny as it seemed to him now, Bilbo realized that, in some way or another, an appreciation for this dwarvish affection had helped to rekindle his longing for errantry. Somehow the image of many-faceted jewels sparkling in deep-delved dwarvish halls had put him in mind of the gemlike stars of heaven. Not that he was ignorant of the dangers of greed—he was old enough to feel the threat of that particular menace. Yet there was something noble and right, he sensed, in the passion of Thorin and his kin for ancestral treasures and the works of their own hands. Strangely enough, that something had revived in him the old desire to walk beneath pines, leap over waterfalls, and sleep under the watchful eye of the moon.

Yes, he remarked to himself as Balin came round the corner of the inn with a pair of heavily laden baggage ponies—this, in some odd way, was how it had all begun.

* * * * *

Few writers can match Tolkien's ability to stir our love of material things.

Yes—I *did* say "love of material things." And I meant it. The delights of eye and ear. The pleasures of touch and smell. The wonder of a world where the luminous stuff of matter ceaselessly assaults the neurons of our fingertips and retinas and eardrums with a never-ending onslaught of textures, colors, and sounds.

The creator of *The Hobbit* is exceedingly adept at bombarding our senses with the marvels of the physical universe. He pours them over us in a flood of poetic description that takes in everything from the glowing grandeur of snowcapped mountains to the perfect circle of a tiny gold ring. And because he does this within the context of an imaginary world, he is able to make us feel as if we were encountering these miracles for the very first time.

That's because Tolkien was an artist of the highest degree. His essay "On Fairy-Stories" is not so much a dissertation on fantastic tales as it is an exposition of the author's personal theory of art and aesthetics: an examination of how the human impulse to make, manipulate, and utilize fits into the Divine Creator's grand design. God, says Tolkien, is the Master Fabricator. People are His apprentices: little "sub-creators" and stewards who flesh out and embellish the work of His hands through their own attempts to mold the raw material of creation.[13] It's quite natural, then, that men and women should find so much fulfillment in the shaping, possession, and enjoyment of *things* of great beauty and worth.

Durin's folk—the race of dwarves—occupy an intriguing place in this scheme. According to the foundational myth of Tolkien's universe (as recounted in *The Silmarillion*), the dwarves were themselves the fruit of a "sub-creative" act. In the First Age of the world, Aulë, smith of the Valar and forefather of all craftsmen and artificers, being impatient for the revelation of the Children of Ilúvatar (elves and men), took the rash step of making "children" of his own. Ilúvatar was less than pleased; but Aulë defended himself with the words, "I desired things other than I am, to love and to teach them.

. . . The making of things is in my heart from my own making by thee."[14] Ilúvatar relented and granted the dwarves a place for their kind beneath the hills and mountains of Middle-earth. And they, like their father before them, became smiths and artisans of incomparable skill: makers and lovers of all things beautiful and bright.

The passion of the dwarves for material things is, of course, a driving force behind the action of *The Hobbit*. It's the catalyst that leads to Bilbo's marvelous adventures in the wild. It's the thread that ties the story together. More importantly, it's the inciting incident in a string of events that have deep and dire implications for the fate of Middle-earth itself. For there would have been no Quest of Erebor and no finding of the Ring had Gandalf not chanced to meet Thorin Oakenshield on the road near Bree, his heart "hot with brooding on his wrongs and the loss of the treasure of his forefathers."[15]

It has to be said, of course, that this dwarvish "materialism" leads in the end to tragedy. But the point to notice here is that it isn't necessarily a negative in and of itself. Indeed, the Bible extols the goodness and delightfulness of God's material creation in many passages of incomparable beauty and grace:

Then God saw everything that He had made, and indeed it was very good. (Genesis 1:31)

And [Solomon] decorated the house with precious stones for beauty, and the gold was gold from Parvaim. (2 Chronicles 3:6)

Command those who are rich in this present age not to be haughty, nor to trust in uncertain riches but in the living God, who gives us richly all things to enjoy. (1 Timothy 6:17)

Like every other manifestation of sin and evil in the world, greed is simply a *good* impulse gone wrong. Tolkien underscores this thought by contrasting "the desire of the hearts of dwarves" with the senseless avarice of the dragon Smaug: "Dragons . . . guard their plunder as long as they live . . . and never enjoy a brass ring of it. Indeed they hardly know a good bit of work from a bad."[16]

To enjoy "a good bit of work"—surely this is one of the greatest of God's gifts; for "nothing is better than that a man should rejoice in his own works, for that is his heritage" (Ecclesiastes 3:22). But to sit on the flashing treasure heap—neither appreciating its glories nor sharing its benefits with others—*this* is the temptation, the vice, the sickness that produces jealousy, strife, war, and death.

But on that night in late April, when he sat in his parlor listening to the songs of the dwarves, Bilbo heard no hint of any such dark and twisted obsession. What came to him instead was a faint echo of the thought of Aulë, the immortal craftsman who longed to make and possess in order that he might give and love and teach. Somehow the prospect of seeing, touching, and experiencing beautiful things—things skillfully contrived and lovingly fashioned for the pleasure of heart and soul and mind—woke up "something Tookish . . . inside him," so that "he wished to go and see the great mountains."[17]

His little brain could never have imagined the terrors, trials, marvels, upsets, and reversals that would flow from this desire.

REFLECTION

Enjoy the treasures of this world, but hold them lightly.

DOOM OF THE DUNDERHEADS

Apparently adventures are not all pony rides in May sunshine, thought
Bilbo. As well he might.

He was lying in darkness in the middle of a great thorn-
bush, his clothes torn, his skin scratched, his stomach knot-
ted with hunger. It could have been worse, of course. He
might have become a partaker in the fate of the dwarves, who
at that moment were lying stretched out in burlap bags beside the dying campfire while three trolls argued about the
best way to cook and serve them. He might even have been
eaten by the trolls himself—*might have*, if the great lumbering
lummoxes hadn't started quarreling over him, and if their
quarrel hadn't degenerated into a full-blown fistfight during
which he'd been kicked into the underbrush and forgotten.

17

To think that the journey had started out so promisingly! Good weather, an easy trot through the outlying farms of the Shire, songs under the open sky. But this pleasant phase hadn't lasted long. Soon the lands around them had grown strange. A heavy rain had set in. One of their pack ponies had fallen into the river, spoiling most of the food supply. After this they had grumbled, groused, and complained until they saw a light—a warm, inviting, reddish light, shining out between the pillars of the tree trunks in the distance—the light of the trolls' cook fire. From that point it was all downhill.

"I say we roast 'em!" one of the trolls was saying. It was the big-nosed, heavy-faced fellow named William. "A bit o' roast dwarf goes down agreeable."

"No time for that," objected Bert, one of William's lumpy-headed companions.

Bilbo, lying atop his bush, reflected dully that there was good sense in this. How long the gang had been quibbling he had no idea, but it seemed to him the night must be far gone by now. And he knew very well that any troll caught above ground at the rising of the sun is immediately turned to stone.

"Boil 'em, then," spat Tom, the third member of the troop. "Boilin's quicker. Easier, too, for a couple o' ninny-hammers like you!"

"Ninnyhammers, is it?" shouted William, clenching his fists.

This led to a protracted dispute, during which the shouts of the trolls rang among the trees while the sky in the east grew lighter and lighter. In the end they agreed to dice and boil their victims. But just as they were sharpening their knives and pulling out their great black pot, a voice that sounded like William's said: "I still say there's nothin' like a bit o' roast dwarf."

Tom turned on William with a glare. "D'yer mean to start all over again?"

"Who, me?" said William. "Start what?"

"Quit yer arguin'!" yelled Bert. And in a trice they were at it again.

The next moment the sun jumped up and the little clearing in the wood fell silent. In place of the three trolls stood three huge granite statues, gleaming dully in the morning light. A tall figure cloaked in gray stepped out from between the trees.

"Dawn take you all, and be stone to you!" cried Gandalf, once again in a voice like William's. For of course it had been Gandalf all along.

* * * * *

According to the psalmist, it's the *fool* who says in his heart "there is no God." It's the *fool* who becomes "corrupt," practices "abominable works," and fails to do good (Psalm 14:1).

The trolls Bilbo and his friends stumble upon in the wilds beyond the Shire are, of course, a bad and wicked lot. It only makes sense, then, that they should also be dim-witted and thickheaded. Their folly, in turn, is characteristically self-defeating—they're constantly fighting among themselves. Not much is required to foil their pernicious plots and thwart their evil designs. All it takes is time and patience—and a cleverly placed word or two.

Counterproductive stupidity is a fairly common quality among giants, ogres, and trolls. These huge and murderous monsters are usually about as bright as a ten-watt bulb in a blinding snowstorm. The immensity of their bodies, like the enormity of their crimes, is offset by the puniness of their pea brains. That's why a yokel like the Brave Little Tailor, unlikely hero of the Grimms' tale, finds it so easy to get the better of two giants he's been ordered to kill. When the tailor climbs a tree and drops a rock on a giant's head, that giant naturally assumes he's been struck by his gigantic companion. It isn't long before *both* giants are lying dead on the ground. Giants, it seems, are dumb enough to be rather good at achieving their own demise. So are Tolkien's trolls.

Like giants and trolls, evil itself is both foolish and self-destructive. This is a thought that surfaces very early in the biblical record. "Of every tree of the garden you may freely eat," God tells Adam, "but of the tree of the knowledge of good and evil you shall not eat, for in the day that you eat of it you shall surely die" (Genesis 2:16-17). Notice that He doesn't say, "*I* will kill you." He simply states, "*You shall surely die.*" That's because the "wages" of sin—its natural, intrinsic, inherently determined consequence—*is* death (Romans 6:23). This means that the man who puts forth his hand to commit wickedness is a plain dimwit. He's like the chowderhead who willingly and knowingly drinks a bottle of shoe polish or ammonia.

Could this have something to do with Jesus' mind-bending statement in Matthew 5:39 about not resisting evil? Was Christ suggesting that evil requires no direct opposition because it is absurd and inane and thus doomed to self-destruct? Of all people, Dietrich Bonhoeffer—the man who eventually became involved in a plot to assassinate the ogre Adolf Hitler—seems to have considered this a distinct possibility at one stage in his life:

> The only way to overcome evil is to let it run itself to a standstill because it does not find the resistance it is looking for. Resistance merely creates further evil and adds fuel to the flames. But when evil meets no opposition and encounters no obstacle but only patient endurance, its sting is drawn, and at last it meets an opponent which is more than its match.[18]

Patient endurance. This, I'd suggest, is the weapon that Gandalf employs so skillfully and effectively in the scene with the trolls. The wizard *could* have rescued Bilbo and the dwarves with an intimidating display of fireworks and blazing lights. He *could* have chosen to overcome his comrades' captors by unveiling his hidden power. He *could* have withdrawn the cloak of age and human frailty and sent the dastards scrambling. Instead, knowing the innate imbecility of trolls, he simply bides his time. He lets the approaching daylight do its work. Now and then he stirs the pot with a well-timed word calculated to enhance the villains' self-imposed confusion. All in all, it's a beautiful picture of the Christian's ongoing struggle against the forces of darkness.

Count Leo Tolstoy is one of the best known proponents of the concept of nonresistance against evil. Though much loved and admired as a novelist, Tolstoy is also highly controversial because of his uncompromising stance on pacifism and nonviolence. While some of his political stands have generated controversy—in his time as well as our own—Tolstoy has something to teach us about the power of goodness, truth, and the Word of God overcoming the asininity of evil. Referring to the threat of political tyranny and oppression, he writes:

All that apparently terrible organization of rude force is nothing in comparison with recognition of the truth, which arises in the heart of one man who knows its force and is communicated by this man to another, just as an endless number of candles are lighted from one. The light need only burn, and this seemingly powerful organization will waste away like wax before the fire.[19]

It's easy to imagine that, in composing these ringing lines, Tolstoy might have been thinking of the words of David: "Do not fret because of evildoers, nor be envious of the workers of iniquity. For they shall soon be cut down like the grass" (Psalm 37:1-2). He may also have been inspired by Solomon's observation that "the turning away of the simple will slay them, and the complacency of fools will destroy them" (Proverbs 1:32). Whatever the source of his thought, he appears to have understood that the gigantic, ogreish, and troll-like threat of the dark realm is, in the final analysis, ephemeral and passing—that given time, it will eventually implode by virtue of its own fatuity and senselessness. "Here," as John the Revelator so memorably puts it, "is the patience and the faith of the saints" (Revelation 13:10).

Martin Luther expresses it this way:

> The prince of darkness grim,
> We tremble not for him;
> His rage we can endure,
> For lo! his doom is sure:
> One little word shall fell him.[20]

REFLECTION

We need not fear a power bent on self-destruction.

Elves they were and remain, and
that is Good People.

—*THE HOBBIT*, CHAPTER 8,
"FLIES AND SPIDERS"

PRETTY FAIR NONSENSE

"This is it! We've found it at last!"

Gandalf was some distance ahead, shouting back at them through the gloaming; and bone tired as they were, Bilbo and the dwarves shook themselves and spurred their ponies forward, anxious to see what the old man had discovered. He was standing beside his horse when they caught up to him, gazing intently over the edge of a steep drop-off, his beard wagging with satisfaction, the tip of his hat tracing crazy circles in the dim blue air. At his feet the rocky ground fell rapidly into a hazy darkness.

"As you can see," he said, "there's a reason why enemies don't often stumble upon the House of Elrond!" With a wink, he swung into the saddle and beckoned to them to follow. "Ride with caution," he advised. "It will be only too easy for the ponies to lose their footing in the fading light."

In later years Bilbo looked back on their descent into the valley of Rivendell as his first step into a larger, lovelier world. Even the air of the place *smelled* distinctly of elves. It made him think of the times—few and far between—when he had encountered their kind wandering by twos and threes in the woods of the Shire: solemn folk with earnest, noble faces and wise, bright eyes. The hobbit sat back and savored the pleasant, drowsy atmosphere as his mount slithered and slipped down the path.

That was when the music first reached his ears. It came rising up from the lower treetops, dancing through the darkness, hanging on the breeze like a meandering mist—a mysterious, madcap melody that raised gooseflesh on his arms and lured him on by the enticement of its fleeting words. He leaned forward in the saddle to listen more closely. But the more he heard, the more perplexed he became:

> *O! Where are you going*
> *With beards all a-wagging?*

It was nothing but nonsense—an erratic jingle in which his own name popped up frequently and the dwarves' grandfatherly whiskers were lampooned in a most disrespectful fashion. Not the sort of thing he'd come to expect from elves.

Bilbo frowned. In the next moment elves suddenly emerged from the woods and surrounded the travelers with gales of happy laughter. Gandalf leapt down among them and began greeting them warmly, embracing some of them as old friends.

"Peace, Good People!" he said at last, lifting a hand to signal silence. "We are grateful for the welcome, but now by your leave we'll be moving along, over the stream to the house of Elrond and some much needed rest!"

"Ah! But be careful of your beard, father!" jeered the elves as Thorin, following Gandalf, stepped out onto the narrow stone bridge that spanned the chattering brook. "You don't want to wet it in the stream!"

"Foolishness!" grunted Thorin, rearranging his cloak and adjusting his hood.

Bilbo forced a cough to cover his laughter.[21]

* * * * *

In the language of Scripture, the word *foolish* can have both a negative and a positive connotation. We've seen the stupidity of evil exemplified in the behavior of the trolls. Now it's time to examine a very different kind of "folly"—the folly of Tolkien's elves.

As I write, two books with sharply contrasting titles have just hit the popular Christian market: *The Importance of Being Foolish* and *Foolish No More*. Mind you, I haven't so much as scanned either one of these books, so I'm in no position to comment on their content; though in view of the merits of the authors (Brennan Manning and Ted Haggard), I think it's safe to assume that *both* are worth a careful read. But if I had to choose on the basis of *title alone*, there's no question which of the two I'd pick. I'd go for *The Importance of Being Foolish* every time.

I have a feeling that the elves would understand.

When I revisited *The Hobbit* after three or four years of immersing myself in *The Lord of the Rings*, I was immediately struck by the difference in tone, color, and atmosphere between the two stories. Bilbo's tale felt noticeably lighter, brighter, and more "fun" than its longer and more ponderous sequel. To a certain extent this was to be expected. After all, *The Hobbit* was written with children in mind, whereas *The Lord of the Rings*, by Tolkien's own admission, grew of its own accord into something "more grown up."[22] Still, there was at least one detail in which the dissimilarity between the two seemed so pronounced as to be almost irreconcilable: namely, the character of the elves of Rivendell.

Descending into the hidden valley, Bilbo and his friends find these elves sitting in trees, contriving irreverent ditties, laughing and joking and mocking dwarvish beards. "*The river is flowing!*" they sing, "*O! tra-la-la-lally . . . The bannocks are baking! O! tril-lil-lil-lolly.*" "Pretty fair nonsense, I daresay you think it," comments Tolkien; and then he adds that "even decent enough dwarves like Thorin and his friends think [elves] foolish."[23]

Some readers may feel inclined to agree. At first glance, these elves appear to be a pretty frivolous bunch. They're quite different from Galadriel, the wise and solemn Lady of the Golden Wood, or her grim and silent consort, the Lord Celeborn. They certainly bear no resemblance whatsoever to the elves of Peter Jackson's film version of *The Lord of the Rings*: the stern and scowling Elrond, the fierce and formidable Haldir, the tranquil and taciturn Legolas.

Tolkien aficionados can accept the scowls and stern words. They know that the history of the elves, as chronicled in *The Silmarillion*, is a *tragic* tale—a story of possessiveness, pride, fratricide, exile, and wandering. They're comfortable with elves who appear to be acquainted with grief and familiar with the wages of sin. But the flighty, "foolish" elves of *The Hobbit*? That's another matter.

Is there a disconnect here? an oversight on the part of the author? I don't believe so. In fact, I can't help feeling that there's a vital message wrapped up in the lighthearted silliness of the Rivendell elves—a message about the "importance of being foolish."

Like the Good People of Elrond's valley, we live in

troubled times. Like them, we dwell under a shadow. We are exiles in enemy territory, hemmed in on every side by darkness and despair. Terrorism and tsunamis, hurricanes and floods, war and senseless suicide bombings—such things have become defining features of the contemporary landscape. That's not to mention the desperate and subtle wickedness that lurks in the deepest regions of every human heart. Can anyone laugh and sing in a world like ours?

The elves of Rivendell say *yes*. And they say so out of a context of hard-earned practical experience. More than any other people in Middle-earth, the elves know what it means to fail. They have fallen from grace and tasted the bitter cost of redemption. They realize what it will take to defeat the Shadow and heal the wounds of the world. And yet they are not above singing in the trees. Indeed, they understand that a certain amount of joyful abandon is *essential* to a life lived in harmony with the truth, however foolish it looks to small and serious-minded folk like Thorin. For to laugh in desperate circumstances and sing in the face of disaster is nothing less than an act of bold and daring faith. It's a sign of salvation to the watching world, evidence of the hope that lies just beyond the fringes of the darkness.

Christians live under the adumbration of just such a bright and shining hope. They follow a Master who lifts their thoughts above the grimness of the present situation and directs their attention to the promise of a better world.

These things I have spoken to you, that in Me you may have peace. In the world you will have tribulation; but be of good cheer, I have overcome the world. (John 16:33)

"Rejoice in the Lord *always*," writes the apostle Paul to the church in Philippi (Philippians 4:4, emphasis added). "Again I will say, rejoice!"—in *any* and *every* circumstance. His words aren't logical. In some ways, they seem completely inconsistent with reason and reality. They contradict the wisdom of the world. And yet, if put into practice, they can become the source of a fragrance not unlike the scent of elvish enchantment that hung above the valley of Rivendell. This is the fragrance of the "foolishness" of Christ: to some "the aroma of death leading to death," but to others "the aroma of life leading to life" (2 Corinthians 2:15-16).

REFLECTION

Live in hope and practice the art of laughter.

Then Gandalf lit up his wand.
Of course it was Gandalf.

—*THE HOBBIT*, CHAPTER 4,
"OVER HILL AND UNDER HILL"

INHERENT
VIRTUE

Things were looking bad for Bilbo and the dwarves. Very, very bad indeed.

"And exactly what were you up to, sitting in my Front Porch?" leered the Great Goblin. His pendulous jowls and bulbous lips flapped loosely as he shook his big ugly head at them. "Are you thieves? murderers? sneaks? spies?"

The hobbit shivered and cast a quick glance around the rough-hewn chamber. It was a dreadful place. The Great Goblin's throne, seat and symbol of his sway over this sunless underground realm, was nothing but a huge flat rock. The cavern where the wretched prisoners stood trembling in chains before him was thick with smoke and leaping black shadows. The only light came from a red fire that sputtered uncertainly in the center of the floor. From a yawning hole at the far end of the chamber rose a confused mingle of faint but ominous sounds: the clinking of chains, the thud of great hammers, the whirring of gears, the reverberating echoes of deep, distant explosions. Rows of pickaxes, mattocks, hammers, and tongs hung ranged along the walls.

The Great Goblin nodded in the direction of an indistinct black shape in the corner: something like an iron bedstead suspended amid a tangle of ropes, spikes, and wheels. "We can make things uncomfortable for you if you won't talk."

"I've already told you," said Thorin, assuming his boldest and most officious manner. "We are travelers. Going east. We mean no harm to anyone."

"No harm, says he?" gurgled one of the goblin guards. "Then what's the meaning of *this*?" With a flourish he drew forth a long elegant blade that flickered with blue fire along its edges.

"Elf-magic!" said one of the others with a wink. "Took it off him in the cave, we did!"

That was enough for the Great Goblin. Instantly he was on his feet, his red eyes bulging out of his malformed head. "Fools!" he screamed. "Not just any elf-magic! That's Biter! The sword of Gondolin! Bane of our folk from ages past!"

Immediately a great din arose in the cavern. The goblins clashed their weapons, stamped their feet, squinted, grimaced, and howled in rage.

"Enemies! Elf-friends!" cried their chief, leaping down from his rock and baring his teeth. "To the pits with them! To the rack! Uncoil the lash!"

He crouched and made ready to pounce upon Thorin. But in that very instant the fire flared up in a fountain of blue and white sparks that trembled in the air for a moment, then winked out, leaving an inky blackness in which Bilbo could not see his hand in front of his face. Without warning, a blue blade flashed out of nowhere, and the Great Goblin fell, pierced to the heart.

A dim light appeared: a faint glimmer bobbing at the tip of a tall wooden staff. In its glow, a face emerged from the surrounding shadows. *Gandalf!*

"We haven't a moment to lose!" he said. "Quickly! Follow me!"

*   *   *   *   *

Magic, enchantment, and displays of supernatural power— they're part of the fabric of fantasy, fairy stories, and myth. Most of us expect the unexpected in imaginative tales, and we're downright disappointed when we don't get it. At least I know *I* am. Why read a fairy tale without mystery and magic? You might as well read a newspaper or an economics text.

Strange, then, that there has been so much confusion and debate about the role of magic in *The Hobbit* and *The Lord of the*

Rings. I suppose it's partly because of the unusual way the subject is approached in these uniquely conceived and carefully constructed tales. For the "magic" of Tolkien's invented world is of a kind you aren't likely to encounter anywhere else.

This is a crucial point for anyone who is genuinely interested in "finding God" in a book like *The Hobbit*. I am speaking of the *biblical, Christian* God: the God who confounds the magicians of Egypt and classes sorcerers with unbelievers and murderers (Revelation 21:8). What do wizards and lighted wands have to do with *Him*?

The episode in the mountain hall of the Great Goblin, where Gandalf uses his wizarding skills to rescue Mr. Baggins and the dwarves, is as good a place as any to stop and ponder this thorny problem. There's an instructive contrast built into the scene. On the one hand, we have Gandalf's pyrotechnics and the flaming blades of the elven swords. Over against these stand the devices and machinations of the goblins—implements of aggression, oppression, and torment. Can we learn anything about the nature of "magic" in Middle-earth by taking a closer look at these two antithetical story elements? I believe we can.

Tolkien has told us that elvish magic is primarily a matter of artistry and self-expression. The elves are not tricksters or shamans but makers and sub-creators *par excellence*. They are children of God who, like their Father, manifest their love for creation by shaping and molding it with an eye for grace and aesthetic appeal. So great is their skill that their craft is infused with the qualities of their souls. Just as the blue flame of an elf-forged sword is a visible manifestation of the inherent virtue of the blade, so the marvelous (and apparently supernatural) works of the elves represent the natural outflow of their innate creative powers: "Their 'magic' is Art, delivered from many of its human limitations: more effortless, more quick, more complete (product and vision in unflawed correspondence). And its object is Art, not Power."[24]

Something similar can be said of Gandalf. Gandalf is *not* a mere "conjurer of cheap tricks." He is in fact a being of a Higher Order: "Gandalf is not, of course, a human being (Man or Hobbit). There are naturally no precise modern terms to say what he was. I would venture to say that he was an *incarnate* 'angel'—strictly an angelos."[25]

When Gandalf cows the goblins with sparks and flames and guides his companions to safety by the light of his marvelous staff, he is not behaving as a magician in the ordinary sense of the word. He does not owe his abilities to esoteric knowledge or occultic lore. On the contrary, he acts the way he does because—well, *because he is Gandalf*. His actions are consistent with his identity and the authority attached to his office. He commands a power that only an "incarnate angel" *could* command. Thus he fulfills his role as "a servant of the Secret Fire, wielder of the flame of Anor."[26]

How different are the diabolical artifices of the goblins! Goblins care nothing for art, beauty, or the "sub-creative" enhancement of the world. Their only concern is to intimidate and dominate. Like the Dark Lord to whom they owe their twisted existence, they crave *power*—power to achieve their cruel and destructive ends: "It is not unlikely that they invented some of the machines that have since troubled the world, especially the ingenious devices for killing large numbers of people at once, for wheels and engines and explosions always delighted them."[27]

This is an important statement because magic—at least the kind of magic we find so uncompromisingly condemned in the Bible—is based on a *mechanical* view of the universe and our relationship to it. In Tolkien's mind, there was a significant link between *magic* and what he liked to call "the Machine":

> By [the Machine] I intend all use of external plans or devices (apparatus) instead of development of the inherent inner powers or talents.
>
> . . . The Enemy in successive forms is always 'naturally' concerned with sheer Domination, and so the Lord of magic and machines.[28]

There is a lesson here for those of us who are on a quest to "find God." For the power of a godly life is not derived from "external plans or devices." It does not come from the manipulation of methods or mechanisms. Prayer and fasting, Bible study and church attendance, evangelism and Scripture memorization—all are necessary and vital in their proper place. But to place too much confidence in them as means of appropriating divine grace is to fall prey to "the Machine." It is to adopt a mechanical or magical approach to the disciple's journey.

God's "magic" is a very different affair. The power of His Spirit dwells in us and flows through us only as we, like Gandalf and the elves, become who and what we were created to be. It's a matter of *essence* and *being*, a question of experiencing rebirth through faith in Christ. This is why Jesus never instructed His apostles to invent strategies or concoct elaborate plans for the evangelization of the world. Instead, He simply said, "You shall receive power when the Holy Spirit has come upon you; and you shall *be* witnesses to Me" (Acts 1:8, emphasis added).

Perhaps this has something to do with the older definition of *virtue*, a word which once meant not only "goodness" but "power."

REFLECTION
Trust God, be yourself, and watch the sparks fly.

IN A TIGHT PLACE

The darkness was oppressive. The air hung heavy with the stench of rotting fish and the musty odor of the flaccid fungi that grow only in lightless places at the roots of the mountains. But it wasn't the thick atmosphere or the fetid stink that made it so difficult for Bilbo to breathe. It was the pounding of his heart and the impatient gurgling and hissing sounds coming from his loathsome opponent in this deadly game.

Curse the creature—this wretched Gollum! he thought, wiping the sweat from his brow. *If only he'd give me . . . just a little more . . .*

"Time!" he squeaked as his adversary stepped from the boat and stretched a skinny arm toward him through the murk. "Time!"

Gollum stopped and stared. "It guesses, preciouss!" he hissed. "It knows!"

But Bilbo hadn't really known. He hadn't even been guessing. Mere chance had brought the right word to his lips at precisely the right moment—for "time" was in fact the answer to Gollum's riddle! He heaved a sigh of relief and ran his fingers through his sweat-drenched hair.

"Another!" Gollum demanded, bending closer with a lean and hungry look in his yellow eyes. "It's got to ask us another quesstion! Yess!"

Bilbo's thoughts ran back to that fateful night when curiosity and his dratted Tookish penchant for adventure had compelled him to throw caution to the wind and join the dwarves in their treasure hunt. If only he'd known then that it would all end like this!

I've never been in such a spot! he groaned inwardly, racking his brain for a good poser. He'd always been good with riddles, but then no one in the Shire had ever threatened to eat him if the game didn't go his way. Besides, he'd already used up all of his best material.

"Ask us!" Gollum pressed.

A bead of sweat dripped from the end of Bilbo's nose. His throat burned. His tongue stuck to the roof of his mouth.

He won't get me without a fight, he thought, planting his feet and fingering the hilt of his sword.

And then, as often happens under the most dire and

desperate circumstances, his mind suddenly and inexplicably skipped away to something completely unrelated: What was it he'd found in the tunnel on his way down to this infernal subterranean lake? His hand crept to his pocket. His fingers touched the cool circle of the little gold ring.

How odd! he said to himself. To think that such a thing should turn up in a place like this! What could it possibly mean?

Before he knew it, the thought had slipped out, and he heard himself voicing his musings aloud: "What have I got in my pocket?"

Gollum scrunched up his face and hissed. Then he clenched his fists and let out a howl of frustration and rage.

"We doesn't know!" he screamed. "Not fair! Not fair, my precious!"

*   *   *   *   *

We all know what it's like to say the wrong thing, take the wrong step, or make the wrong decision in the heat of an anxious moment. You could almost say it's the story of the human race.

But have you ever tripped up under pressure and somehow fallen in the *right* place? Stumbled in the darkness and landed on your feet? When your back was against the wall and you were so flustered, frightened, or exhausted that you hardly knew what you were doing, did you ever blurt out something crazy, take a desperate swing, or flash on a random thought, only to find that you'd blindly put your hand on the key to the entire situation?

Something of that sort happened to Bilbo Baggins as he stood trembling by the shore of Gollum's underground lake, fighting for his life in a dangerous battle of wits.

The riddling contest narrated in chapter 5 of *The Hobbit* used to present something of a conundrum for me. It was troubling to think that our hero may have won the competition by bending the rules—a disturbing possibility, since "the riddle-game was sacred and of immense antiquity, and even wicked creatures were afraid to cheat when they played at it."[29] After all, the query that stumped Gollum wasn't technically a riddle. It was merely a question: "What have I got in my pocket?" A simple, straightforward question, to which the unhappy creature couldn't possibly have known the answer. Wasn't Gollum right to call foul? I had an uneasy suspicion that he was.

But then it occurred to me that Bilbo hadn't intended the question as a riddle at all. On the contrary, it just popped out of his mouth while he was thinking about something else. His mind played a trick; and almost before he knew what was happening, Gollum had seized upon his words and was angrily and reluctantly conceding defeat. It wasn't exactly a legitimate victory, but it gave Mr. Baggins the edge he so desperately needed.

IN A TIGHT PLACE

Is there a point to all this? Does Bilbo's fortunate brain lapse have any significance beyond the narrative necessities of this particular episode? The more I've pondered this question, the more I've become convinced that the answer is yes.

In trying to persuade the dwarves to engage Bilbo's services as a "burglar," Gandalf had reflected on the mettle of the Shire-folk by saying, "You have to put these Hobbits in a tight place before you find out what is in them."[30] It's a recurring theme in *The Hobbit* and *The Lord of the Rings*: There's more to these unassuming halflings than meets the eye. It's also a message that most of us have heard reiterated many times before in other contexts. True nobility emerges only under great pressure. You have to squeeze the grape to get the juice. When the going gets tough, the tough get going.

All true enough. But the interesting thing is that this is *not* the lesson that emerges from the story of Bilbo's encounter with Gollum. To be sure, Mr. Baggins was in a *very* tight place as he groped in the darkness for a puzzler to save his skin. And yes, there is a sense in which the crisis he faced tested his resourcefulness and resolve as they'd never been tested before. But in the end, it was neither resolve nor resourcefulness that kept the hobbit from becoming Gollum's next meal.

What, then, was it? It was . . . well, *something else*. Something that had nothing to do with ability, cleverness, character, or resolution. Bilbo's thoughts wandered, some words tumbled out, and suddenly he found that the tide had turned—not only in his personal favor, but in a way that would change the entire course of the history of Middle-earth.

I consider this one of the most intriguing episodes in the entire history of *The Hobbit*. The incident is at once so absurd and yet so pivotal that it can't help but raise a series of interesting questions. Was there a method to the madness? Do we discern some sort of "Intelligent Design" at work beneath the surface of Bilbo's mindless stammering? Could the *something* have been *Somebody*? The tale itself never gives us a direct answer. But it's a hypothesis we'll want to revisit before closing the book on the story of Mr. Baggins's adventures in the wild.

"The preparations of the heart belong to man," writes Solomon, "but the answer of the tongue is from the LORD" (Proverbs 16:1). In some odd way, Bilbo's riddle game with Gollum makes me think of this wise and ancient saying. For at the moment when he needed it most, the hobbit's mind slipped from his conscious control, and his tongue uttered words that he hadn't really intended to speak. Where did those words come from? Hard to say. But perhaps they were a part of Someone's hidden plan.

What about you? Is it possible that, in the midst of a thousand blunders and errors and random chances, happy mistakes of this sort have been dropping quietly and unobtrusively into *your* life? Is it conceivable that, in such moments, Someone else has been holding the reins of your destiny firmly in hand?

It's a question well worth asking. Because it's easy to miss the randomly scattered and arbitrarily disguised miracles that lurk in the hidden corners of life's tight places.

REFLECTION

Unexpected things come out when the squeeze is on.

A PIECE OF FOLLY

Bilbo raised his face from the rocky floor and propped himself on one elbow. Gollum, a vague silhouette against the greenish glow of his own luminous eyes, was already disappearing down the passage. Apparently the creature hadn't even seen him lying there. How was it possible?

I'm rid of him at any rate! the hobbit told himself. But then another thought struck him like a well-aimed punch to the gut: He was alone in the goblin tunnels and didn't know the way out! For better or worse, that foul sneak Gollum represented his one and only hope of escape. Cautiously he got up and began to follow at a safe distance.

"Curse the Baggins!" he heard Gollum wheeze. "We hates

it!" Bilbo trembled, for there was a murderous edge to the creature's voice. "We knows what it's got in its pocketses! And if the goblinses get it, we'll never be safe! They'll catch us unawares! We won't see them coming! *Gollum!*"

So that's it! thought Bilbo, turning the ring on his finger. *A magic ring! A ring of invisibility!* Perhaps there was a chance after all. . . .

He followed his unwitting guide into a section of tunnel where crosscurrents of air bespoke the presence of intersecting side-passages. Bilbo ran his fingers along the wall until they slipped off into empty space. At that very moment he heard Gollum whisper: "This is it—yes! One left. . . . One right!"

Slowly they inched their way forward, Gollum counting under his breath all the while, until at last they reached the sixth opening on the left. There the creature stopped before the entrance to a diverging tunnel, lifted up his nose, and sniffed.

"Ssss! The back-door! But we durstn't go—not without the birthday present! Goblinses are there! We smells them!" With that he plopped down in the middle of the opening, heaving and shaking, his miserable head cradled in his thin spidery hands.

Now what? Bilbo squirmed. Gollum had led him to the exit, and still he couldn't get out—the weeping, whining wretch was blocking the path! The hobbit gritted his teeth and put a hand to the hilt of his sword. He took a tentative step away from the wall.

Immediately Gollum's sobbing ceased. His head shot up. His eyes flickered green. He rose to a crouch and poised himself to spring.

There's nothing else for it, thought Bilbo, biting his lip. *It's my skin or his! Kill or be killed!* Carefully he began to draw the blade from its sheath.

And then he stopped. For all at once a vision rose before his mind's eye: a vision of what it meant for this lonely sufferer to lose the only thing he had ever loved. He stood there eyeing the creature, poor and unarmed as he was. *No,* he thought. *I can't.*

The sword slipped back into the scabbard. In the next instant Bilbo was running for all he was worth, leaping, clearing the shape in the doorway, tearing down the tunnel.

Behind him rose a scream that chilled his blood—a thin, piercing scream that reverberated down the corridor, pulsing with pain and the promise of revenge.

"Baggins! Thief! We hates it! We hates it *forever!*"

* * * * *

You've probably heard the old adage "Nice guys finish last." Much as it hurts to have to say it, there's a lot of truth to this heartless maxim—at least in terms of the harsh realities of the world in which we live. All too often, "survival of the

51

fittest" is more accurate as a description of human relations than of biological processes.

I believe this is why so many of us struggle to accept Christ's instructions with regard to the proper handling of hostile, hateful people. "Love your enemies," He says in the Sermon on the Mount. "Bless those who curse you, do good to those who hate you, and pray for those who spitefully use you and persecute you" (Matthew 5:44). This follows hard on the heels of an even more outrageous demand: "I tell you not to resist an evil person. But whoever slaps you on your right cheek, turn the other to him also" (Matthew 5:39). In yet another place, Jesus sums it all up with this simple but daunting mandate: "Be merciful, just as your Father also is merciful" (Luke 6:36).

So thoroughly do these directives defy everyday logic and common sense that most Bible commentators would rather tell us what they *don't* mean than what they *do*. Jesus wasn't questioning the legitimacy of self-defense, they assure us. Jesus never meant to suggest that it's wrong to stand up for yourself. He certainly wasn't asking anyone to become a doormat. Fair enough. But what *was* He trying to say?

Let's be honest: This is an extremely difficult concept to understand. Yet for all its difficulty, Bilbo Baggins seems to grasp it in a flash as he stands in the gloom of the goblin-tunnel looking down at the mean-spirited, self-consumed creature called Gollum.

Bilbo, we must remember, is in a desperate situation. He *has* to escape if he is to survive, and Gollum is standing in his way. Not only that, but there is a menacing light in the creature's eyes. Under the circumstances, it would be so easy to stick the nasty stinker in the dark and be done with it. Who could blame him? But somehow or other, Bilbo can't bring himself to strike the blow. At the critical moment, a sudden insight into Gollum's despondency and despair—a capacity to see matters from *his* point of view—fills the hobbit with an overwhelming sense of pity and stays his hand.

In hindsight, it's easy to see the positive long-range ramifications of Bilbo's act of mercy. Ultimately, his compassion becomes the linchpin upon which the fate of Middle-earth turns. For Gollum is the one who, in the end, brings about the destruction of the One Ring and ensures that the quest of the Ring-bearer succeeds. His actions prevent the world from falling into even greater darkness. Gandalf foresees all this: "My heart tells me that [Gollum] has some part to play yet, for good or ill, before the end; and when that comes, the pity of Bilbo may rule the fate of many."[31] And so it does.

But the thing to notice here is that Bilbo does not know this at the time. He can't possibly know it. He shows mercy *for mercy's sake alone.* And for all he can tell, his tenderheartedness might turn out to be a fatal mistake. Given the murderous gleam in Gollum's eye, there is every reason to suppose that the wretch will stop at nothing in his quest to regain the "precious." It is conceivable that, as a reward for his kindness, Bilbo will eventually be hunted down and throttled in his sleep. But then it's precisely this element of ignorance and incalculable risk that makes his deed so meaningful.

Tolkien understands this: "Of course, [Gandalf] did not mean to say that one must be merciful, for it may prove useful later—it would not then be mercy or pity, which are only truly present when contrary to prudence."[32]

Elsewhere Tolkien speaks in a similar fashion of Frodo's compassion for Gollum (in *The Lord of the Rings*), which in many ways is the direct result of Bilbo's: "To 'pity' [Gollum], to forbear to kill him, was a piece of folly, or a mystical belief in the ultimate value-in-itself of pity and generosity even if disastrous in the world of time."[33]

A piece of folly. Contrary to prudence. Disastrous in the world of time. Phrases like these are hauntingly reminiscent of the experience of some of the greatest saints in the history of the Christian church. People like Stephen, who, while being stoned to death by an angry mob, did not curse or fight or fret, but raised his eyes to heaven and prayed, "Lord, do not charge them with this sin" (Acts 7:60). Or Edmund, King of the East Anglians, who, when confronted with the threat of Danish invasion, "threw away his weapons, desiring to imitate the example of Christ"—and lost his kingdom, his life, and his head as a result.[34] Or Jim Elliot and Nate Saint, who expired at the end of Waodani spears, unwilling to fight back because that would have betrayed their gospel witness. Or Jesus Himself, who hung on the cross and prayed, "Father, forgive them, for they do not know what they do" (Luke 23:34).

No doubt about it. There *have* been times in the lives of God's people when the "nice guys" finished last. When gentleness and forbearance did not turn out to be as profitable and beneficial as they did in the case of Bilbo Baggins. At least not in the short term.

But what is "disastrous in the world of time" is not necessarily so in the perspective of eternity. For in the economy of God's kingdom, we have the assurance that acts of mercy, foolish though they may appear at the moment, are endued with a strange power: the power to open doors to the mysterious operation of sovereign grace.

When those doors swing open and the light of divine mercy flows in, then at last we will know that we have truly "found God"—or that *He* has found us—in a way that passes all understanding and denial.

REFLECTION

A tender heart is a marvelously impractical thing.

> *"The Eagles! The Eagles!"* he
> shouted. *"The Eagles are coming!"*
>
> —*THE HOBBIT*, CHAPTER 17,
> "THE CLOUDS BURST"

ON EAGLES' WINGS

Just one kettle of fish after another! Bilbo sighed. *First the frying pan, then the fire! Why couldn't I have had the sense to stay at home?*

He was up in a tree, of all places. Bilbo Baggins, a hobbit of the Shire—a respectable, sensible hobbit who was petrified of heights and couldn't understand how Bree-folk managed to live in two-story houses. In a tree!

But it was worse than that. Much worse. For not only were the pine needles poking him in the eyes and getting tangled in his hair. Not only did he feel as if he might at any moment roll off the branch he'd chosen for his perch and tumble to the ground. On top of everything else, there were big orange flames licking the tree trunk and tickling the soles of his feet. And wolves—the fearsome Wargs—slinking from shadow to intervening shadow. And goblins clashing their weapons and singing rude songs to taunt their helpless quarry. To think that he'd left his comfortable hole in the Shire for *this!*

The dwarves, of course, had been treed as well. Gandalf too. Even now Bilbo could see the wizard standing on a bough near the top of a tall pine, a lean, shadowy figure in a pointed blue hat, his craggy bearded face and bristling brows flashing out of the darkness in the intermittent glow of the fireballs he was tossing down upon their enemies. It was a brave defense he was making, and Bilbo knew that if anyone could stave off the wolves and goblins, it would have to be Gandalf. Still, he had his doubts. Even now the flames were singeing the hair on his poor bare toes.

All at once from out of the sky came a sound like a mighty rushing wind. Bilbo looked up and saw the treetops lashing to and fro against the stars. It was difficult to tell in the dark, but he thought he could discern huge winged shadows swooping down from the heavens and wheeling above the forest. At the same time he heard a great shout and saw Gandalf, in one last burst of effort, heaving himself to the very summit of his shuddering pine. The wizard raised his wand and made as if he would jump down into the midst of the goblin warriors. But he never got the chance.

The next thing Bilbo knew, Gandalf was soaring skyward,

gripped in the talons of a gigantic eagle. The great birds seemed to be everywhere now, screaming out a warning to the Wargs and mountain orcs, picking the dwarves out of the branches and bearing them skyward.

"Quick!" shouted Dori from somewhere above Bilbo's head, his voice nearly lost among the howls of the wolves and the cries of the goblins. "Grab my legs or you'll be left behind!"

A moment later Bilbo was swinging madly above the tree-tops, clinging for dear life to the dwarf's stout knees, watching in amazement as the flames and the forest and the towering plumes of smoke dwindled into the distance below.

* * * * *

It's the semimonthly meeting of our informal writers group, the Stinklings (a name we chose in self-deprecatory tribute to our literary heroes),[35] and the talk has turned to *The Lord of the Rings*. Paul, ever the discriminating critic, is pointing out a potentially fatal flaw in the premise of Tolkien's epic.

"Think about it," he says. "If the eagles can fly into Mordor at the *end* of the quest to rescue Sam and Frodo from the eruption of Mount Orodruin, why couldn't they have flown into Mordor at the *beginning*? Why didn't Elrond and Gandalf get *them* to drop the Ring into the Cracks of Doom in the first place? Why send the hobbits at all?"

Al raises an eyebrow. Kurt nods judiciously. *Interesting question*, I think.

Anybody who is even moderately familiar with the lore of Middle-earth knows what Paul had in mind. Time after time, in crisis after crisis, the eagles "save the day" by appearing over the horizon at precisely the right moment. The scene at the climax of *The Return of the King* is an unforgettable example. So is the episode recounted above—the one in which the great birds unexpectedly rescue Bilbo and friends when they've been treed by wolves and goblins (*The Hobbit*, chapter 6).

Paul seemed to have put his finger on something. Why didn't the Wise realize from the very beginning that the eagles represented the answer to all their problems? How could Tolkien have failed to make such an obvious connection? These were bothersome questions. I felt that the author of *The Lord of the Rings* was too meticulous to have overlooked a difficulty as glaring as the one my friend appeared to have uncovered. What's more, I believed that he was too fine a writer to stoop to shopworn literary tricks like the deus ex machina. At least he wouldn't have done so without a good reason. I thought that if I searched hard enough, I'd be able to discover what that reason was. I wasn't disappointed.

There's a pattern to the eagle rescues that dot the pages of Middle-earth history. This pattern points to a certain wonderful and startling conclusion. It suggests that we might be justified in seeing these majestic birds as a beautiful and powerful image of divine *grace*. *Free* and *sovereign* grace. This in turn seems to supply the solution to Paul's disturbing puzzle. Because grace isn't something you can control. Like Bilbo and Frodo, you can only look up and receive it with a sigh of relief. You can only give thanks and shout, "Hallelujah!" when it swoops down to snatch you out of a hopeless impasse. To experience grace is to be left speechless and awestruck—not wondering how you might have found a way to take advantage of it earlier on.

How did I arrive at this conclusion? Simple. I came to the realization that the eagles of *The Hobbit* and *The Lord of the Rings* are no ordinary birds. They are in fact the Eagles of Manwë[36]— Elder King, chief of the Valar, viceroy of Ilúvatar, and ruler of Arda.[37] Within the economy of Tolkien's world, they can be compared to "the eyes of the LORD" that "run to and fro throughout the whole earth, to show Himself strong on behalf of those whose heart is loyal to Him" (2 Chronicles 16:9). They function as executors of the divine will—extensions of a Love that defies mortal comprehension and reaches down to men and elves from a place beyond the boundaries of the world.[38]

There's a very good reason, then, why the eagles couldn't possibly have been conscripted to take the Ring to Mordor. These birds simply aren't available for hire—not even by the likes of Master Elrond. They can't be manipulated or controlled. They come and go solely at the beck and call of their master, the king of all the earth. And *he*, for reasons best known to himself, seems to have decided that the salvation of the West cannot be achieved until Frodo and Sam have trod the path of sorrow and suffering for a little while.

In the same way, no one, not even a wizard like Gandalf, could *compel* the eagles to rescue Thorin and Company from the Wargs and goblins of the Misty Mountains. Here, too, Tolkien seems to whisper that deliverance from certain doom and defeat is always a matter of pure, unmerited grace—the same grace that seeks us when we'd rather not be found, goes before us at every moment of our lives, prepares paths for our footsteps without our knowing it, and draws us irresistibly toward the loving heart that beats at the center of all things.

For by grace you have been saved through faith, and that not of yourselves; it is the gift of God, not of works, lest anyone should boast. (Ephesians 2:8-9)

Is it possible to catch the Eagles of Manwë and persuade them to do your bidding? Can you use them to serve your own agenda or advance your own cause? Will they plunge to your rescue simply because *you* feel you've had enough?

Might as well ask if you can coerce a butterfly to land on your shoulder—or bottle and sell the grace of the living God.

REFLECTION

God reserves the right to intervene in our lives as He chooses.

*"Beorn may be your friend,
but he loves his animals as his
children."*

—*THE HOBBIT*, CHAPTER 7,
"QUEER LODGINGS"

CREAM AND HONEY

Not since the fortnight they'd spent in the House of Elrond had Bilbo and the dwarves been treated to such hospitality. But it was hospitality of an unfamiliar and ambiguous kind; for while they were warmly welcomed and lavishly fed, they were also reminded at every moment that they had now come in earnest to the untamed lands of the eastern Wild.

The food was simple but hearty: bread and butter and honey. The entertainment was stirring but unsettling: hair-raising tales of the dark and dangerous woodland. The steep-roofed hall, redolent of pitch and resin and smoke, echoed with the bleats and neighs and barks of the table servers—a flock of sheep and a troop of ponies and dogs. As for the host, he was a veritable bear of a man, whose black beard flowed with mead and whose tangled hair flew in every direction as he held forth from the head of the table in a booming baritone. But then *this* host was a tale-and-a-half in himself.

Gandalf had warned them to be careful of Beorn. He called him by a name Bilbo had never heard before— *skin-changer*—and said that he possessed the power to assume at will the form of a man or a great black bear. Beorn lived alone, removed from human society, keeping extensive gardens and barns full of horses and cattle, with whom he conversed in a growling, guttural tongue. Around his great wooden house stood rows and rows of big bell-shaped beehives. Honey and cream were the main staples of his diet.

"Don't do anything to anger him," the wizard had said. "For though he is generous and openhearted, he is also a law unto himself and will brook no nonsense from the likes of you. Above all, avoid giving offense to any of his creatures. They are his family—brother, sister, parent, child—and he would as soon break your heads as allow you to mistreat them!"

Bilbo could not help remembering these words when he lay down for the night on the mattress of straw that Beorn had spread for him at the side of the hall. Beyond the walls of the house the wind was up and howling. Inside, the dwarves had gathered around the embers in the fire pit and were chanting songs about the dragon and the wide lands that lay between them and the Lonely Mountain.

> *The wind was on the withered heath,*
> *but in the forest stirred no leaf. . . .*

With a sigh, Bilbo lay back and stared up into the black shadows beneath the rafters. And as he looked, it seemed to him that the pillars of the hall were beginning to sprout branches and leaves, and that great horned owls were roosting and hooting among the topmost boughs. The wind moaned and whistled down the smoke hole. The hobbit's eyelids grew heavy.

Suddenly the door slammed with a *bang!* Bilbo bolted up, all ears and pounding heart. Beorn was nowhere to be seen. But out in the farmyard there arose a scratching and a snuffling, like the noises made by some great prowling beast.

Bilbo shivered. *Skin-changer,* he thought. Then he lay down and tried to console himself with thoughts of breakfast— bread and butter with cream and honey.

* * * * *

The charm of Middle-earth lies largely in its believability. And its believability is in many ways a function of the meticulous care with which its inventor has designed and defined it. It's a logical, sensible world—a place of clearly delineated boundaries and distinct categories. Accordingly, most of the folk you'll find tilling its fields, mining its hills, or wandering its roads can be easily identified as representatives of certain familiar types: dwarves or hobbits; men or elves; ents, orcs, trolls, or wizards.

But there are a few odd characters in out-of-the-way corners who defy such classification. I'm thinking of two in particular: old Tom Bombadil, the jolly sprite who haunts the willowy banks of the Withywindle;[39] and Beorn, the fierce skin-changer of Wilderland.

Beorn stands outside all systems of taxonomy and codification. He is, in a word, unique. To Bilbo and friends, he is a happy enigma: gruff, short tempered, and aloof, yet an invaluable source of nurture in time of need (if handled properly); an unfailing ally to his friends, an implacable terror to his enemies. At one moment he sits among his houseguests, telling tales and quaffing mead like one of the regulars at the Green Dragon Inn. At another he slips away to roam the trackless wastes as an unsympathetic creature of the night. Beorn lives in harmony with the patterns and rhythms of the untamed lands—indeed, he is a part of those patterns and rhythms himself.

It's not hard to see in Beorn a living, breathing image of J. R. R. Tolkien's heartfelt reverence for creation. For the author of *The Hobbit* was a passionate lover of the natural world. Biographer Daniel Grotta-Kurska tells us that Mabel Tolkien "managed to instill in her older son an 'almost idolatrous' love of trees, flowers, and nature"[40]—an affection that finds poignant literary expression in the bucolic serenity of the Shire. Conversely, Tolkien's resentment of the road builders, developers, and despoilers of rural Oxfordshire[41] comes through loud and clear in his disparaging descriptions of the goblins, who love "wheels and engines and explosions,"[42] as well as the traitorous wizard Saruman, who "does not care for growing things, except as they serve him for the moment."[43] Clearly, the architect of Middle-earth believed that nature is something to be cherished, respected, and treated with the utmost care.

This is a profoundly Christian conviction. As any student of Scripture knows, the biblical writers frequently exult in the unspoiled beauty of creation. Many times they convey what can only be called a reverential respect for nature's untamed power and might. Ultimately they go beyond this to make the astonishing claim that, except for the face of Christ Himself, the natural order is the place where God's character is most plainly revealed—a thought too often neglected in the history of western Christendom.

The heavens declare the glory of God; and the firmament shows His handiwork. (Psalm 19:1)

Since the creation of the world His invisible attributes are clearly seen, being understood by the things that are made, even His eternal power and Godhead. (Romans 1:20)

Nor is it merely nature in the broad sense of the universe at large that the Bible celebrates as a manifestation of God's goodness and love. The creatures themselves—plants, animals, and monsters of the deep—are accorded a similar place of honor. When the Lord wants to expose the narrowness of Job's human-centered perspective, He calls his attention to the mysterious life cycles of wild animals: "Do you know the time when the wild mountain goats bear young? . . . Does the hawk fly by your wisdom? . . . Can you draw out Leviathan with a hook, or snare his tongue with a line which you lower?" (Job 39:1, 26; 41:1). Jesus points to the "birds of the air" and the "lilies of the field" as illustrations of divine providence (Matthew 6:25-30). John portrays Christ as both a Lion and a Lamb (Revelation 5:5-6).

Such declarations are not to be taken lightly. For while it is true that mankind in its unfallen state was granted "dominion" over creation (Genesis 1:28), this does not mean that we have free rein—particularly in our present sin-tainted condition—to abuse the earth's resources for our own selfish ends. On the contrary, if our mind-set is truly biblical, all of our interactions with God's creatures will be characterized by an attitude of solemn fear and attentive love. "A righteous man regards the life of his animal, but the tender mercies of the wicked are cruel" (Proverbs 12:10).

That's because nature, like Beorn the skin-changer, can be both a nurturing friend and a terrible foe, a welcoming host and a ravaging bear. It all depends on how you approach her. If we believe what God says about His intentions for the blissful interdependence of the created order—if we truly long for the day when "the wolf also shall dwell with the lamb . . . and a little child shall lead them" (Isaiah 11:6)—then we must learn to "respect the particular goodness of every creature" and "avoid any disordered use of things which would be in contempt of the Creator and would bring disastrous consequences for human beings and their environment."[44]

That's the only way to get on nature's good side—and to taste the flowing sweetness of her cream and honey.

REFLECTION

To love God is to cherish the things He has made.

UNATTAINABLE
VISTAS

Bilbo shivered and slid down off his pony. It was already late afternoon, and a cold wind was rising. Before him loomed the densely tangled wall of the forest of Mirkwood, stark and darkly green in the mellow light of the sinking sun, its boughs and branches creaking and clacking ominously with the erratic stirring of the breezes. There would be no more traveling that day. They would camp here, under the eaves of the wood, and begin their trek beneath the forest canopy at dawn.

"Well then, Mr. Baggins," said Gandalf, dismounting beside him and clapping him on the shoulder. "How do you like the look of it?"

"Like?" answered Bilbo. "I can't say that I do. The sight of it fills me with dread—dread of all that I have never known and cannot see . . . everything that lies hidden within the boundaries of the wood's shadowy borders. The world is a bigger place than I realized, Gandalf. I see now that it contains many things beyond the grasp of my puny imagination."

Gandalf laughed. "If that is your view, then I would suggest that your imagination is keener and more far-reaching than most! But there will be plenty of time for such musings later on. At the moment, my friends, the first order of business is to unload your gear and say good-bye to these fine ponies. For Beorn will not permit you to take them into the wood; and as I've already warned you, it would be extremely unwise to anger him by playing fast and loose with any of his beloved creatures."

"And what about you?" growled Thorin, stepping between Bilbo and Gandalf and jutting his bearded chin up into the wizard's face. "Will *you* also be sending back that high-stepping horse of yours?"

"No," Gandalf answered good-naturedly. "I will *not* be sending him back. I will be returning him personally! For as you must have guessed, this is where we part."

Here there arose a general groaning, grumbling, and complaining among the dwarves.

"Just when a wizard would have been most helpful, too!" exclaimed Balin.

"How do you expect us to get on without you?" moaned Bombur.

"There's no sense in arguing!" said Gandalf, seating himself on a rock and pulling out his pipe. "We've been over this ground before. There is a situation developing in the South— a long, long way from here—that requires my attention. As Mr. Baggins has so rightly perceived, there is more to this wide world than you people appear to have dreamed of. The tides of time and fate do not await the settling of your personal affairs before sweeping on to their determined end. Now let's hear no more about it!" With that he struck a spark from his tinderbox, lit his pipe, and began puffing away in silence.

That night Bilbo lay bundled in his bedroll, looking up into the cold and starry expanse of the heavens, listening to the indefinable moanings of the vast dark forest.

In the South, he thought, his mind eddying around the vortex of mystery concealed within those three small words. *I wonder where that is . . . and why he is going . . . and what it all means. . . .*

* * * * *

Have you ever felt what Bilbo felt? Have you ever been overwhelmed by a sense of the unbounded and unknowable vastness of the universe? Taken aback by a glimpse of the unplumbed depths of your own invisible soul and the uncharted reaches of the subconscious mind? Stunned and alarmed at the unfathomable mystery of God Himself—a God big enough to create the cosmos and intimate enough to comprehend the thoughts of every man, woman, and child ever born?

I recall as a boy going with my parents on selected Sunday afternoons to visit an elderly aunt of my dad's. There wasn't much for a kid like me to do at Auntie Day's house, so I used to spend a lot of time on the sofa, staring at her knickknacks and *objets d'art*. I remember in particular a pair of cast-iron angels that sat on a mahogany end table: two curly-headed cherubs, one playing a harp, the other pounding an anvil with a hammer.

For me, there was something haunting about these two dark figures. I didn't fully understand what they were supposed to represent; and it was partly for this reason that the sight of them filled me with an inexpressible awe, a dim premonition of the interminably galleried and echoing halls of heaven. I came to regard them as symbols of eternity. Lying in the darkness in the middle of the night, picturing their smooth foreheads and placid eyes, I would wrestle with the concept of absolute endlessness and the prospect of everlasting life. Such thoughts caused me to tremble and shiver; and yet they also allured and attracted me. Thus it was that in these midnight meditations I took some of my earliest steps toward a larger and more wondrous world.

The same sort of attraction hovers around the storytelling of J. R. R. Tolkien. To an important degree, the fascination of a book like *The Hobbit* is linked to things that we *never see* and *do not understand*—elements of the tale that lie just over the narrative's edge. Take for example Gandalf's mysterious errand in the South. When the wizard leaves Thorin and Company at the verge of Mirkwood and rides off into the distance, we, like Bilbo, can't help wondering, *How far south is South? Exactly* where *is he going? And what's he going to do when he gets there?* We have only to hear those two little words—"away South"—and we fall immediately under the spell of "far away places with strange sounding names,"[46] distant lands forever receding beyond the blue horizon.

Tolkien understood this. That's why he designed his web of stories as "a Frameless Picture: a searchlight, as it were, . . . on a small part of our Middle-earth, surrounded by the glimmer of limitless extensions in time and space."[47] Such value did he attach to this indefinable "glimmer" that he questioned (at least for a time) the wisdom of releasing his *Silmarillion*, the mythic iceberg of which *The Hobbit* and *The Lord of the Rings* are only the tip. How would the reader's enjoyment of his previously published works be impacted, he wondered, if he were to unveil mysteries hitherto referenced only by way of fleeting hints and allusions?

Part of the attraction of [*The Lord of the Rings*] is, I think, due to the glimpses of a large history in the background: an attraction like that of viewing far off an unvisited island, or seeing the towers of a distant

> city gleaming in a sunlit mist. To go there is to destroy
> the magic, unless new unattainable vistas are again
> revealed.[48]

As the author of *The Hobbit* knew very well, these "unattainable vistas" are what keep readers of fantasy hungering and thirsting for more. Eliminate them, resolve the tension of the hidden mysteries they conceal, and there is a very real danger that the enchantment of the tale will be reduced to a heap of ashes and dust.

As in Tolkien's fiction, so in life—it is the mist at the edge of the "frameless picture" that entices the traveler to leave his comfort zone and launch out into unexplored territory. It's what the spectator *can't* see that drives him to push for a place at the front of the crowd. It's the impenetrable cloud of shekinah glory that captures the worshipper's imagination and keeps her endlessly questing—pressing forward, searching, seeking a better vantage point from which to gaze upon the dimly perceived beauties of the Promised Land.

This is a thought that comes persistently to mind whenever I find myself faced with unanswerable questions about the nature and character of God, when hurricanes and AIDS epidemics and the paradox of divine sovereignty and human will pass before me in a long and bewildering parade. I try to use such moments as opportunities to embrace the marvel of *mystery*, to remember that the intensity of my desire for the

Lord is in many ways directly proportional to what I *don't* understand about Him, that I am drawn to Him largely because I can't completely figure Him out.

"For My thoughts are not your thoughts, nor are your ways My ways," says the LORD. "For as the heavens are higher than the earth, so are My ways higher than your ways, and My thoughts than your thoughts." (Isaiah 55:8-9)

"Eye has not seen," writes Paul (quoting Isaiah), "nor ear heard, nor have entered into the heart of man the things which God has prepared for those who love Him" (1 Corinthians 2:9). Here is a promise sufficiently veiled in glory to entice even the most timid of hearth-loving hobbits away from his pipe and bowl. And isn't it exactly what we should expect of the Father of all things, the One who dwells in unapproachable light? For "a God comprehended is no God" at all.[49]

REFLECTION
What we don't know is every bit as important
as what we do know.

RELUCTANT LEADER

Darkness, discouragement, and despair. That's what life had become for poor Mr. Baggins over the course of the past several weeks.

Or was it months? He could no longer tell. For him, existence and consciousness had long since dissolved into an endless blur of eating, sleeping, creeping, hiding, lurking, pilfering, and staying in touch with the incarcerated dwarves (always, of course, with the aid of his ring). It was as if the wheels of the world had ceased to turn the moment he entered the underground labyrinth of the Elvenking's palace. And to think that this interminable dreariness was actually an improvement over the dark and dangerous days they'd spent trekking through the lightless forest of Mirkwood! A black adventure, indeed! Except for the time he had climbed a tree to scout out their position, Bilbo had seen neither sun nor sky since setting foot in Mirkwood.

It was in this dejected frame of mind that the hobbit found himself tiptoeing invisibly down the dungeon corridor to the cell where Thorin was being held captive. Lightly he tapped at the heavy wooden door and put his ear to the keyhole.

"Baggins?" the voice was dry and harsh with disuse. "Back so soon?"

"Yes," he answered. "I've delivered the message."

"To all twelve?"

"Every single one. No capitulation, I told them."

"Good!" The dry voice crackled with satisfaction. "They agreed, I take it?"

"To a dwarf. No volunteering information. Above all, not a word about the treasure. Nothing at all until—"

"Until the miraculous Mr. Invisible Baggins finds a way to spring us from this hole! As I'm sure he will!"

Bilbo groaned inwardly and pressed his forehead against the door. "Right."

"So what is the next step in your plan?"

"*My* plan?" Bilbo swallowed. "The others all asked the same thing. But I have no plan."

"Oh, but you will. You will! We have faith in you! So did

Gandalf, as I now see. He was right, of course. As usual. A most remarkable burglar you've turned out to be!"

Gandalf! Bilbo wished with all his heart that the wizard could be with him now! Gandalf would have known what to do. He would have brought out his magic staff, there would have been a blinding flash, as in the cave of the Great Goblin, and all would have been well. But Gandalf was long gone. Probably at the other end of the world by now. If anything was to be done, it was obvious that Bilbo would have to do it himself. He leaned against the stone wall of the corridor and slumped to the floor.

If only I'd stayed at home, he thought, *with the fire burning and the kettle singing and a meat pie cooling on the windowsill!*

*   *   *   *   *

At one time church tradition called for nominees to the office of bishop to decline with the words *nolo episcopari*: "I do not wish to become a bishop." Only the man capable of repeating this formula and really meaning it was considered fit for the task of shepherding the faithful.

Originally this seems to have been something more than just a polite formality. When the apostle Peter, sensing the nearness of his own death, chose Clement to succeed him as overseer of the church in Rome, Clement tried to beg off: "I knelt to him, and entreated him, declining the honor and the authority of the chair."[50] St. Anselm (eleventh century) seems to have been of a similar frame of mind: According to some accounts, he had to be held down, his fingers pried open, and the episcopal staff forced into his hand when he was made Archbishop of Canterbury. Chad (Ceadda), Bishop of York (seventh century), was unperturbed when critics challenged the legitimacy of his appointment: "If you decide that I have not rightly received the episcopal character," he said, "I willingly lay down the office."[51]

Clement, Anselm, and Chad—three of the greatest leaders in the history of the church. But they were also three of the most *reluctant*. Indeed, it seems safe to assume that the tradition of *nolo episcopari* is at least partly attributable to the influence of their legacy.

In the secular realm, too, it has long been recognized that the person best suited to exercise authority is the one who wants it least. That's why the early Romans worshiped the memory of Lucius Quinctius Cincinnatus (born about 519 BC), the legendary statesman who was *twice* called upon to assume the (temporary) office of dictator and *twice* returned to his farm when the state of emergency had passed.[52] Cincinnatus was clearly a very different sort of person than Julius Caesar, that shrewd politician who preferred to hold on to absolute power once it was in his grasp. Thomas Jefferson might have been thinking of Caesar when he wrote, "Whenever a man has cast a longing eye on [public office], a rottenness begins in his conduct."[53]

During the course of his adventures, Bilbo Baggins emerges as a leader in the style of Clement and Cincinnatus. He does not seek, nor did he expect to receive, a position of preeminence among his traveling companions. Their confidence and respect are thrust upon him through circumstance alone. It is in the midst of the battle with the giant spiders that the dwarves first begin looking to Bilbo for guidance. Then when they find themselves imprisoned in the dungeons of the Elvenking, they trust *him* to come up with a plan of escape. Later, when they stand staring down into the darkness of the dragon's lair, it is Bilbo who offers to use his ring to creep inside and spy on Smaug. It's at this point that the narrator is able to say, "[Bilbo] had become the real leader in their adventure."[54]

But Bilbo, like St. Anselm, is not enthusiastic about this turn of events. He operates according to the principle of *nolo episcopari*. When the mantle of authority falls upon his shoulders, his one wish is to find a way out from under it. He *knows* that he isn't up to the challenge of guiding the dwarves through the wilderness, delivering them from dangers, destroying the dragon, and liberating the treasure. *That* is a job for a wizard, not a furry-footed, yellow-waistcoated, middle-aged bachelor from the Shire! But the wizard is unavailable, and Bilbo has to do the best he can. In the event, he comes through with flying colors.

Why should this be so? What is the germ of wisdom

hidden within the kernel of *nolo episcopari*? Why in the world should a soul who is faithful and good and talented and true be reticent to take up the staff of the shepherd? And why should we, as the people of God, be especially on the lookout for potential leaders who can only be dragged into the job kicking and screaming? At least two reasons come to mind.

The first has to do with humility—something with which Mr. Baggins, due to his small stature and lack of experience, is liberally endowed. "Pride," says the Scripture, "goes before destruction, and a haughty spirit before a fall" (Proverbs 16:18). This is especially true in the case of the individual who is entrusted with responsibility for the well-being of his or her fellows. For overconfidence leads to carelessness, and carelessness to false steps; and a false step, bad as it is on its own account, can be disastrous if it entails the fate of other people. Consider the example of Moses. As long as he doubted his own ability (Exodus 4:10), Moses was filled with a power and wisdom that could only have come from above. But when he allowed himself to become swollen with a sense of his own importance, he fell into error and forfeited his chance to enter the Promised Land (Numbers 20:8-12).

The second reason is more subtle. A true leader shies away from his calling because he knows there's nothing in it for *him*. He understands that the perils, the anxieties, and the sleepless nights will be endured *not* for the sake of personal gain, but for the benefit of somebody else. In other words, he realizes that genuine leadership is a matter of service and self-sacrifice; and that's always a bit uncomfortable.

You know that the rulers of the Gentiles lord it over them, and those who are great exercise authority over them. Yet it shall not be so among you; but whoever desires to become great among you, let him be your servant. And whoever desires to be first among you, let him be your slave. (Matthew 20:25-27)

Nolo episcopari! Or, as one clever commentator translates it, "Not me, Jack."[55] Such is the cry of every heart that perceives its own frailty and knows its true condition in the sight of the living God. And such is the person God can use most powerfully to feed His sheep and tend their wounds. For distrust of self is the first step toward dependence upon Another, and "the fear of the LORD is the beginning of wisdom" (Psalm 111:10).

REFLECTION

True leaders endure their lot for the sake of others.

So you see Bilbo had come in the end by the only road that was any good.

—*THE HOBBIT*, CHAPTER 10,
"A WARM WELCOME"

A FORTUNATE MISTAKE

"Don't leave the path!"

Those were Gandalf's final instructions, the very last (and apparently the most important) words he had spoken to Bilbo and the dwarves before wheeling his horse around and riding away to attend to pressing business elsewhere.

Bilbo, worn out, wet through, and slightly seasick atop the bobbing barrel raft, sighed with remorse. *Wouldn't you know it would turn out this way?* he thought. He shut his eyes and pictured the wizard galloping off into the west. "Whatever you do," he had shouted back at them as they stepped into the shadows of the forest, *"don't leave the path."* Yet that was exactly what they had gone and done.

Not maliciously, of course. Not out of any wish to be rebellious or refractory. It wasn't even a case of lapsed memory: Never once had they been unmindful of the terrors that haunted the trackless wastes of Mirkwood. Still, their decision *had* been conscious and willful. It was a question of sheer necessity. In the end, hunger and the hope of finding a meal had enticed them off the road and driven them into the wood.

The misfortunes they'd suffered since that moment were proof enough of their folly. Darkness, spiders, and venom. Sickness, despair, and captivity. Even now, Bilbo couldn't help wondering whether any of the dwarves had actually survived their escape from the elf-king's dungeons. *Probably all drowned in those leaky barrels by now.*

"Don't I know it!"

Bilbo looked up at the sound of a voice. It came from one of the elves who stood along the bank, poling the mass of barrels downriver.

"Never any letup in the river traffic nowadays," the elf was saying. "And the Lake-men expect *us* to maintain the banks and towpaths!"

"That's right," rejoined one of his companions. "Let the raftsmen of Mirkwood do it! But I remember a time when things were quite different."

"Before the rise of the Shadow in the South," said another. "Before the rains and the floods and the swelling of the marshes in the East. Before the path was washed out."

Path washed out? Bilbo pricked up his ears.

"No more caravan travel along *that* route," agreed the second elf. "But business is business, and the trade must go on. So it's all up to *us*."

The hobbit couldn't believe what he was hearing. Had Gandalf really been unaware of all this? *"Stick to the path!"* he had told them—apparently in dead earnest. Beorn had said the same thing. But if these raftsmen were right, *that* road would have led them all to a watery dead end!

The sun was high now, glittering on the surface of the water. Away to the east a cloud-covered peak shimmered like a dim and distant vision above the red-gold horizon— the Lonely Mountain! Bilbo shaded his eyes against the glare.

"Off with you, then, my bouncing barrels!" shouted the first elf, giving the raft a great shove with his pole. "And may luck go with you to Lake-town!"

*　*　*　*　*

The Hobbit, Tolkien tells us, was vaguely conceived—at least in the beginning—as a "children's" fairy-story.[56] However imprecise this design may have been in its earlier stages, the author appears to have carried it through with careful attention to detail and a high regard for the mandates of tradition. For Bilbo's story contains a number of well-worn fairy-tale conventions.

FINDING GOD in THE HOBBIT

Among the most obvious and noteworthy of these is the fairy-tale *prohibition*: something that somebody is solemnly exhorted *not* to do but invariably ends up doing anyway—in spite of threats, sanctions, and warnings of dire consequences.

The Seven Dwarves tell Snow White not to open the door to *anybody* under *any* circumstances—a directive she disregards *three* times, nearly to her own undoing. Bluebeard gives his young bride the run of the castle except for one small room; and she, quite naturally, risks her life to find out what's inside. "One thing you must promise me," says the White Bear (a prince under an evil spell) to the heroine of "East o' the Sun and West o' the Moon." "Do not talk alone with your mother, else you'll bring bad luck on both of us." This, of course, is exactly what she does—and loses her enchanted lover as a result.

Sound familiar? It should. Stories like these are essentially reruns of the drama of Eden: "Of every tree of the garden you may freely eat; but of the tree of the knowledge of good and evil you shall not eat, for in the day that you eat of it you shall surely die" (Genesis 2:16-17). This, in a nutshell, is the history of the entire human race—and the tale of every individual human heart.

The Hobbit features a fairy-tale prohibition of its own. At the edge of the grim and forbidding forest of Mirkwood, Gandalf leaves Thorin and Company with a single word of warning and advice: *Stick to the path!* A simple assignment. But like the protagonists of myths and fables the world over, Bilbo and the dwarves just can't seem to pull it off. They try, but everything works against them. When at last their food supply runs out and they catch a glimpse of elves feasting in the wood, the gnawing in their bellies drives them over the edge: "They all left the path and plunged into the forest together."[57]

But that's not the end of the story. For in *The Hobbit*, the old fairy-tale prohibition takes on a surprising twist. Though Bilbo and his companions, like Snow White, disregard their mentor's instructions, and though, like the lass in "East o' the Sun and West o' the Moon," they suffer hardship as a result, there nevertheless comes a point in the narrative when the significance of their error suddenly emerges in a whole new light. Overhearing the talk of the raftsmen on the Forest River, the hobbit makes an astounding discovery: Leaving the path, it seems, was *the very best thing* he and his companions could have done, Gandalf's sober warnings notwithstanding. Had they not taken this ill-advised step, in fact, they would almost certainly have fallen into a bog and never reached their goal.

For Bilbo, this is a moment of wonder. For the reader, it can be yet another image of the miracle of divine sovereignty and providence. We've encountered this theme before. It surfaces again and again in the imaginary tales of J. R. R. Tolkien. But it makes its appearance at this particular juncture in a most remarkable way.

Not only are Thorin and Company shown grace *in spite of* their folly, as in the encounter with the trolls. Here, their disobedience actually becomes the *means* of their deliverance. Not only do they find that unsought misfortunes, trials, and sufferings can work together for good, as in the case of their run-in with the goblins.[58] On this occasion, even willful neglect is turned into a blessing. Not only does an unthinking blunder bring beneficial results, as it did at the conclusion of Bilbo's riddling game with Gollum. In this instance, even intentional *sin*—if we may use that word—becomes an indispensable thread in the tapestry of the overall plan.

Is this possible? Do things ever work this way in what Tolkien calls "the primary world"—the world of our everyday lives? Does God's grace actually extend *this* far?

We know that it does. If you doubt it, just take a look at the genealogy of Jesus (Matthew 1:1-17). It's not just that this catalog of Christ's earthly forebears includes some pretty notorious sinners—faithless and bloody kings like Ahaz (v. 9) and the idolatrous Manasseh (v. 10). It's also that in several places a *specific act* of disobedience or licentiousness—for example, Judah's incestuous liaison with Tamar (v. 3; see Genesis 38) or David's adultery with Bathsheba (v. 6; see 2 Samuel 11)—appears to have become an essential link in the human chain that led to the Savior's birth.

What an incredible God we serve! A holy God who hates sin, but who is creative and innovative enough to weave it into His all-embracing, merciful plan. A God whose gracious design "to give [us] a future and a hope" (Jeremiah 29:11) *cannot* be thwarted by the worst we can do! Need we look any further for reasons to put our trust in Him?

"How unsearchable are His judgments and His ways past finding out!" (Romans 11:33).

REFLECTION

God can use even our sin to accomplish His purposes.

*"Never travel far without a rope!
And one that is long and strong
and light. . . . They may be a help
in many needs."*

—THE LORD OF THE RINGS, BOOK II,
CHAPTER 8, "FAREWELL TO LORIEN"

A BIT OF ROPE

Bilbo lay panting on the mountainside, staring up at the clouds, listening to the happy talk of the dwarves as they passed the golden cup of Thror from hand to hand.

"Here's to Mr. Baggins!" said Thorin, passing the gleaming treasure to Gloin.

"A redoubtable burglar and an excellent hobbit!" said Balin, beaming.

Bilbo glowed with gratification.

"And his burgling's just begun!" Gloin grinned, running a finger along one of the cup's sleekly curving handles. "There's heaps more treasure where this came from!"

At this Bilbo sat up and frowned. He hadn't the slightest

intention of going back into the dragon's lair. He opened his mouth to say so—but never got the chance.

"What was that?" shouted Dori as the mountain shook and a shower of stones came skittering down the slope above their heads. They all jumped to their feet. A moment of tense stillness followed; then came a deep rumble, a muffled roar, and the sound of a great bellow echoing up the tunnel behind the secret door.

"Smaug wakes!" whispered Nori. "He misses the cup!"

"Now see what you've done!" said Oin, scowling across at Bilbo. "You've gone and roused the dragon's wrath!"

Again Bilbo opened his mouth to protest. But in the next instant the night sky was ablaze with red light. Tongues of flame licked the crest of a distant ridge. The hobbit turned and grabbed the nearest dwarf—it happened to be Bifur—by the sleeve.

"Quick!" he shouted. "Everyone into the tunnel!"

But Bifur pulled away, his eyes wide with alarm. "We can't! Bombur and Bofur—they're still down in the valley with the ponies and our supplies!"

Bilbo's heart sank. A groan went up from the rest of the dwarves. "They'll be killed!" wailed Dwalin, wringing his green hood between his hands.

"Not if we can help it!" said Thorin, stepping into their midst and tossing the great cup down into the grass. "It's not gold we need at a time like this. It's a bit of rope!"

Rope! thought Bilbo. *Of course!* And in the next instant they were all frantically digging through their packs, drawing out long brown coils of the precious stuff. Over the edge of the precipice they paid them out, thirty, forty, fifty ells and more.[59] Bofur and Bombur, who had seen the dragon's fire, were already dragging bags of food and gear to the base of the cliff, shouting up at them through the din among the rocks.

"Up with you!" grunted Thorin as another spout of flame, closer this time, scattered the darkness—and over the cliff-edge tumbled Bofur with three bundles of stores. "Now, once more!" shouted the chief dwarf. "With a will!" Then they all heaved and pulled, their eyes bulging, their cheeks puffed up like balloons, and up came poor fat Bombur, panting and trembling, his pale face a picture of terror and confusion.

After that they fled, squeezing into the narrow tunnel and shutting the door—all but a crack. The next instant the mountain shuddered and the grassy bay outside their hiding place burst into flame.

* * * * *

"Got rope?"

This is a question that pops up again and again, generally at fairly strategic moments, in Tolkien's tales of Middle-earth. In fact, it recurs frequently enough to make one wonder: Is there a point to all this talk about rope?

Kneeling on the brink of the enchanted river in the dark forest of Mirkwood, Bilbo catches sight of a small boat resting against the farther bank—the troop's only hope of crossing the sleep-inducing stream in safety. "Can any of you throw a rope?" asks Thorin. Several stout lengths are produced and, sure enough, after a few unsuccessful attempts, the boat is snagged and drawn across the water.[60]

Filled with excitement at having discovered the secret door in the side of the Lonely Mountain, Thorin and Company make their way up the precipitous path, each with "a good coil of rope wound tight about his waist"—the only gear they are able to carry with them. With the same ropes the dwarves haul up provisions from the valley, while fat old Bombur remains below with the ponies, convinced that the lines will not support his weight. "Luckily for him," comments the narrator, "that was not true, as you will see."[61]

And so we do, in the breathtaking scene renarrated above. With barely a moment's notice, Thorin and the others must pull Bombur and Bofur to safety when the dragon emerges from his lair, seeking the thief who has absconded with his golden cup. Once again the task is accomplished by means of rope.[62]

In *The Lord of the Rings*, Sam, setting out from Rivendell, checks his pack and discovers he's forgotten rope. "You'll want it, if you haven't got it," he tells himself.[63] Fortunately, several coils are supplied in Lorien; and, as one of the elves there predicts, they prove to be "a help in many needs."[64] "What a piece of luck you had that rope!" says Frodo after safely descending a sheer cliff-face in the rocky waste of the Emyn Muil. "Better luck if I'd thought of it sooner," observes Sam.[65]

Rope may be the most underestimated of all mankind's considerable technological innovations. Loud praises have been sung in honor of the forgotten hero who designed the wheel. But what about the genius who invented rope? Through a long and tedious process of spinning and twisting, counter-twisting and braiding, the rope maker takes thousands of small and insubstantial fibers and unites them into a single strand of sufficient strength and length to restrain a horse, bear a man's weight, or rig a tall ship. An impressive achievement. But who ever stops to think about it?

With ropes men have raised the pyramids, circumnavigated the globe, and scaled Mount Everest. With ropes, we are told, an army might actually hope to pull down a stronghold (2 Samuel 17:13). Rope came in handy for the four men who had to lower their paralytic friend through the roof in order to get him to Jesus (Mark 2:4; Luke 5:19). Paul must have thanked God for it when he realized that the only safe way out of Damascus was through a hole in the city wall (Acts 9:23-25). When a tempest arose and battered the ship in which the apostle was being transported to Rome, it was with ropes (Greek *boetheiai*—literally "helps") that the sailors undergirded the vessel in an attempt to strengthen it against the pounding waves (Acts 27:17).

Amazing, isn't it, how often the thing we overlook, underestimate, or fail to think about until the very last minute turns out to be salvation itself? "You'll want it if you haven't got it," said Sam, and he was right. Sam of all people knew the value of a bit of rope, yet he *still* left Rivendell without it. Thorin and Company brought some along, but they didn't dream there would come a moment when a length of rope would be of far greater value to them than all the treasure in the world. Jewels bedazzle and gold beguiles, but in a pinch, life itself may depend on a strand of twisted hemp or nylon—as Bombur discovered. At such times, it's good to know that "a threefold cord is not quickly broken" (Ecclesiastes 4:12).

Perhaps this is one of those reflections that requires a brief disclaimer. I apologize if I seem to be twisting or stretching my material to make a point. We all know that Tolkien wasn't trying to teach or moralize when he described Bombur and Bofur's last-minute escape from the wrath of the dragon. His only purpose was to weave a well-told tale. And yet, as I've allowed my own thoughts to interact with the imagery of the story, I've come away with a feeling that there *is* a lesson to be drawn from this vividly narrated episode.

Among other things, I can't help thinking that the grace of

God is a lot like a bit of rope. It's the thing we tend to forget when we get caught up in the busyness of everyday life. We bury it at the bottom of our pack. We leave it at home when we go out into the world. Our memory of its worth pales as we contemplate the glitter of temporal treasures. But in a crisis—in a foxhole, or on the edge of a crevasse, or in the jaws of a fire-breathing dragon—it's the one thing we'd give the world itself to possess. "You'll want it if you haven't got it."

What a joy to realize that we need never face such a dilemma! To know that those who really want it can *always* have it! For His mercy to us is unfailing, and His grace is a lifeline for all who are in need. And "how shall we escape if we neglect so great a salvation"? (Hebrews 2:3).

REFLECTION
God's grace is the narrow strand on which
all our hopes depend.

This of course is the way to talk to dragons.

—*THE HOBBIT*, CHAPTER 12,
"INSIDE INFORMATION"

MORE RIDDLES IN THE DARK

"Come out, thief, and help yourself! You needn't lurk in the shadows!"

The dragon's deep voice rumbled from one end of the high-vaulted hall under the mountain to the other. Bilbo, remembering the fiery terrors of the previous night, stood trembling in the red glare of the monster's sweeping gaze. What a piece of luck to have a ring of invisibility! It was standing him in good stead now.

"I have no interest in treasure, O Smaug!" the hobbit ventured to reply, poking his unseen head out of the tunnel's narrow opening. "I came only to find out whether the tales of your greatness tell true. I see the bards have not exaggerated."

"Indeed?" There was a self-satisfied gleam in Smaug's glittering eye. "And what do you call yourself, my fine, fair-spoken plunderer of the possessions of others?"

Bilbo smiled to himself. "I am the clue-finder and the web-cutter," he replied. "I am the stinging fly and the friend of eagles. I come from under hill and over hill. I soar through the air and walk unseen!"

"Impressive," said the dragon, a plume of noxious smoke trailing upward from each nostril. "But it was your *name* I requested. Not your fine-sounding titles."

"To be precise, O Greatest of Calamities," said Bilbo, "you asked me *what I call myself*. And I answered truly. I call myself Ringwinner and Luckwearer."

Bilbo, of course, had heard enough about dragons to appreciate their wily ways. He wasn't about to give this one the advantage by revealing his true name. Besides, he was in his element now; he had reason to fancy himself something of an expert in the art of riddling.

"I am the Barrel-rider," he went on. "I am the one who drowns his friends and pulls them alive again from the water!"

"Friends?" sneered the dragon. "Hmm! *Dwarvish* friends, unless my nose deceives me. A faithless, tricky lot—don't you find? I see they've fooled *you* into doing all their dirty work! Not as clever as you seem, I guess. I'll wager you never see so much as a penny for all your trouble!" And the hall rang with his laughter.

At this Bilbo faltered. Odd as it sounded, old Smaug was only echoing a thought that had passed through his mind many times before. But he pushed his feelings down and answered in a quavering voice, "You are mistaken, Smaug! Gold is not our main concern. We come for vengeance."

"Vengeance!" roared the dragon. "You and whose army? Don't you see my scales? They're thick as shields! I am invulnerable!"

"Even—" Bilbo squeaked—"even *underneath*?"

Again Smaug laughed and rolled over on his side. "There!" he said. "How do you like my impenetrable diamond waistcoat?"

"Stunning!" cooed Bilbo. But to himself he said, *My father was right! Every worm* does *have his weak spot!*

For there in the hollow of the dragon's left breast was the thing he had been hoping to find: a patch of soft skin the size of the hearth rug at Bag-End.

* * * * *

How are you at riddles?

They're not just child's play, you know. Because we live in a world of dragons. A dark, dangerous, *fallen* world, where perils sleep beneath the hills and where twisted motives, hostile intentions, and sly traps are the order of the day. A world where "not all have faith" (2 Thessalonians 3:2) and where the good and the godly never lack for antagonists. You have to be canny and clever—maybe even a little crazy—to get by in a world like that. You have to know how to *talk* to the dragon if you're going to spend much time knocking around inside his lair.

Mr. Bilbo Baggins seems to understand this concept. He appears to have grasped the point that you can't be too careful when conversing with malevolent serpents. He realizes, among other things, that it is extremely unwise to tell a dragon your real name, because your name is a symbol of your essential, inner self. And to expose your heart and soul heedlessly and needlessly to powers that don't have your best interests at heart is to play the fool.

But Bilbo's comprehension goes deeper than this. He also knows that the best way to talk to a dragon is in *riddles*; for "no dragon can resist the fascination of riddling talk and of wasting time trying to understand it."[66] In his encounter with Smaug, the hobbit demonstrates that one of the most effective strategies for throwing an enemy off his guard and buying yourself the chance you so desperately need is to *keep him guessing*.

Jesus took a similar tack in dealing with some of the dragons *He* had to face during His time on earth—dragons like unbelief, apathy, and stubborn resistance to the truth. He didn't challenge these serpents to a knock-down, drag-out battle. He didn't always speak plainly, laying it all out for everyone to see, friend and foe alike. Instead, knowing the human heart as intimately as He does (John 2:24-25), He spoke shrewdly and winsomely to the dragon that lurked in its depths. He said things calculated to stir its curiosity. He revealed the fullness of His glory only to a select few. To the rest He talked in riddles—*parables*, as the Gospel writers call them.

To you it has been given to know the mysteries of the kingdom of God, but to the rest it is given in parables, that "Seeing they may not see, and hearing they may not understand." (Luke 8:10)

Incredible as it seems, the purpose of Jesus' parables was *not* to clarify or illustrate, as we are often led to believe. The purpose of the parables, by Christ's own account, was to *obscure* and *conceal*. In other words, the parables, like Bilbo's riddles, were designed to throw the dragon off balance and keep him guessing. A wild and daring plan, to be sure; but in the end it worked like a charm.

Of course, the obscuring function of riddles can sometimes cut both ways. In some instances, Jesus made intriguing statements for the purpose of drawing unbelievers out and enticing them to dig deeper—as in his conversations with Nicodemus (John 3) and the woman at the well (John 4). In his book *Blue Like Jazz*, Donald Miller describes how he and a few Christian friends decided to set up a "Confession Booth" at Reed College's annual Ren Fayre, a bawdy celebration of on-campus hedonism, indulgence, and general all-round decadence. The really unusual thing about their idea was that they *weren't* planning to solicit tearful acknowledgments of guilty wrongdoing from the pagan revelers. Instead, as Miller's friend Tony explained it,

> We are going to confess to them. We are going to confess that, as followers of Jesus, we have not been very loving; we have been bitter, and for that we are sorry. We will apologize for the Crusades, we will apologize for televangelists, we will apologize for neglecting the poor and the lonely, we will ask them to forgive us, and we will tell them that in our selfishness, we have misrepresented Jesus on this campus.[67]

The result of this acted parable—this riddle in the flesh—was that some people's preconceived notions about Christians were shaken to the core. Students who assumed they had these narrow-minded, right-wing bigots pegged went away scratching their heads. Visitor after visitor to the "Confession Booth" said things like, "It's really cool what you guys are doing," and "I'm going to tell my friends about this." A number of them wanted to hug the "confessors" before going away. Several came back to find out more about what they believed. "I think that night was the beginning of change for a lot of us," Miller concludes.[68]

This is the way to talk to dragons. *This* is an example of what it means to speak to the world in disarming riddles. It's a tactic believers desperately need to reclaim in this postmodern era of hostile indifference to the gospel. For as Bilbo understood so well, it can be disastrous to reveal too much to an unfriendly opponent, to "cast your pearls before swine" (Matthew 7:6), as Jesus expressed it. But if you can draw the dragon out with a little game of cat and mouse—if you can get him puzzling about your *true* name and wondering who you *really* are in your heart of hearts—you may eventually persuade him to lower his guard and show you his weak spot.

That's when you can go in for "the kill"—with patience, humility, and an attitude of self-sacrificial love.

REFLECTION
Circumspect's the word.

GRIM BUT TRUE

A hint of gold. A splash of pale ocher on the distant mountainside. A hopeful-appearing blush at the edge of the horizon. That's how it all began.

The few folk who happened to be out strolling along the quays in the cool of the evening saw it clearly through the gap in the hills at the far side of the Long Lake. It was like the glow of a great forge, they thought, the way it flashed out and hung trembling on the heights, then surged and faded, only to flare up again after an interval of blackness.

Before long, people were standing in knots along the railings, peering and pointing into the night, whispering that the King under the Mountain, having returned to his halls, must be hard at work refining his silver and gold. A few recited snatches of the song they had sung in celebration of Thorin's arrival in Lake-town:

His wealth shall flow in fountains
And the rivers golden run.

Soon their voices were rising above the rooftops in a paean to the advent of halcyon days and flowing streams of wealth. But the prudent among the townsfolk simply smiled and took a more practical view. "If the dwarf *is* a king," they said, "it's high time we began to reap some of the benefits of his return!"

"King under the Mountain!" muttered a grim-voiced, grim-faced man who stood apart in the shadows. "The dragon is the only mountain-king we've ever known. And if that isn't the glow of *his* fire, then I'm a codfish."

"Not a codfish, Bard!" they laughed. "A wet blanket! Always looking for the dark cloud behind the silver lining—that's you!"

But the laughter and the singing quickly gave way to an uneasy silence. For no sooner had the water at the end of the Lake flushed red-gold, in apparent fulfillment of the old prophecy, than the true source of its gilding became all too obvious. Everyone saw it at the same time: an ominous spark of flame approaching from the direction of the Mountain, speeding through the darkness, growing rapidly against the backdrop of the cold white stars.

One by one they turned to Bard, fear flickering over their faces in the play of the fiery light. But Bard was not there to see the look of dread in their eyes. Already he was running, shouting, pounding at the door of the Great House, rousing the Master of the town.

"The dragon! The dragon!" they heard him cry as a sudden blast of hot air ruffled their hair and fluttered the edges of their cloaks. "Cut the bridges! To arms!"

And now trumpets were sounding and soldiers' feet were thundering along the quay. Somewhere close at hand a thatched roof burst into flame. Bard caught up his great yew bow and strode to the water's edge.

*   *   *   *   *

Bard of Lake-town, descendant of Girion of Dale, is one of the most memorable figures in the entire history of *The Hobbit*. Bard is a great hero in Middle-earth—perhaps one of the greatest of them all. For it is Bard, not Bilbo or Thorin or Gandalf, who ultimately brings down the terrible serpent Smaug. In all the annals of Tolkien's imaginary world, only the ill-fated Túrin Turambar, slayer of the formidable worm Glaurung, shares with Bard the distinguished title of Dragon's Bane.[69]

Interesting thing about Bard. It is not merely his strength or bravery that earns him a place among the luminaries of his time. He is bold and decisive, to be sure. But to a great extent he owes his courage and determination to a certain frame of mind.

To put it bluntly, Bard is a *grim* man. A realist. A cynic. The sort of person who sees the glass as half empty rather than half full. He has a glum way of looking at life and reading the signs of the times. And yet, for all his gloominess, Bard is also faithful and true. In fact, it's possible to argue that his steadfastness is a direct by-product of his skepticism.

Bard is the sort of fellow who, though respected among his friends, nevertheless leaves people shaking their heads at the pall of pessimism that seems to hang over him like a thundercloud. Folk complain that he has a penchant for digging up trouble where there is none to be found. "You are always foreboding gloomy things!" they say. "Anything from floods to poisoned fish. Think of something cheerful!"[70]

But Bard isn't particularly talented in the area of thinking cheerful thoughts. That's because he recognizes the world for what it is: a beautiful but terrible place, a garden of delights laced throughout with evil and cruelty and hidden perils. And seeing the world as he does, Bard does not shrink from calling a spade a spade. He realizes that the townspeople will scoff if he questions their visions of silver and gold flowing down the river from the Lonely Mountain. But he also knows that a dragon haunts those heights; and when a red-gold glare comes rippling over the surface of the lake, he thinks it unwise to leave that fire-breathing enormity out of his calculations.

Bard is not an unfamiliar character. He's a bit like Cassandra, the prophetess of Greek myth, who was fated always to speak the truth but never to be believed. When Cassandra warned the people of Troy that the wooden horse was a ruse, they laughed and called her a "doomsayer." Then they proceeded to drag the ominous thing straight into the heart of the city. Few survived to admit what a terrible mistake they'd made.

Bard is also reminiscent of Micaiah, that redoubtable Old Testament prophet concerning whom King Ahab of Israel said, "I hate him, because he does not prophesy good concerning me, but evil" (I Kings 22:8). When summoned to advise the king and his colleague, Jehoshaphat of Judah, as to the wisdom of a campaign against the Syrians, Micaiah lived up to his reputation by predicting a disastrous defeat. "Didn't I tell you so?" Ahab complained to his fellow monarch. Unfortunately for him, Micaiah's prophecy proved to be as true as it was grim.

Even among the disciples of Jesus we find examples of men like Bard: curmudgeonly sorts whose cynicism proved integral to their tenacious loyalty to the cause of Christ. Take Thomas, the "doubter." His hard-headed realism became the foundation of a faith tough enough for him to carry the gospel to India and endure a martyr's death. Then there's

Nathanael—that old sourpuss who couldn't find a thing to say at his first meeting with the Master except, "Can anything good come out of Nazareth?" (John 1:46). Apparently it never occurred to Jesus to censure the man's sarcastic attitude. On the contrary, He commended him for his straightforwardness: "Behold, an Israelite indeed, in whom is no deceit!" (John 1:47).

In the same way, Bard comes off as a hero not only *in spite of* his grim outlook, but precisely *because* of it. In the end, the Lake-men have good reason to be thankful for his dark sense of foreboding. Because if it weren't for Bard, Smaug would have caught them completely unawares. Without his dire warnings of approaching danger, they would never have found the courage to resist the onslaught of the dragon's fury.

Do you know someone like Bard? If so, remember the dragon and resist the temptation to instruct your friend in the virtues of a sunshiny disposition—at least until you've heard the *reasons* for his skeptical outlook. Listen first and lecture later. You may be glad you did.

And if you're a bit like Bard yourself, don't lose heart. Don't buy into the notion that your faith is somehow inferior to that of the Pollyannas and positive thinkers. If promises of health and wealth and rivers of gold strike you as a bit far-fetched—if you doubt the motives of those who cry, "'Peace, peace!' when there is no peace" (Jeremiah 6:14)—then by all means say so. Stay sober and alert (1 Thessalonians

5:6). Speak the truth as you've been granted to see it. The rest of us are counting on you.

After all, it's a grim world out there.

REFLECTION
"There lives more faith in honest doubt, believe me, than in half the creeds."[71]

*Then Bilbo, not without a shudder,
not without a glance of longing,
handed the marvellous stone to
Bard.*

—*THE HOBBIT*, CHAPTER 16,
"A THIEF IN THE NIGHT"

HANDING IT OVER

Winter was definitely drawing on. Bilbo could feel its approach as he sat there in the middle of the November night, warming and drying himself at the big campfire before the Elvenking's pavilion. He felt it in his bones and in the deepest places of his heart: a sense of cold foreboding that had been growing in him all through the dull, gray days of Thorin's stubborn and fractious resistance to the overtures of the elves and the Lake-men. He knew that time was running out. If the chief dwarf didn't come to terms with his adversaries soon, the siege and the snows would be the death of them all. Well then, perhaps he could be *forced* to come to terms.

It just so happened that Bilbo had the means of applying a bit of force. Whether through luck or Fate or random chance, he had been granted a marvelous gift—the gift of *leverage*. Reaching into his damp coat pocket, he touched the little bundle of rags that lay there and pictured the glittering wonder that slept within its dark folds. The Arkenstone of Thrain. The most precious, beautiful, and dazzling gem the hobbit had ever seen. Thorin, he knew, valued it above a river of gold. Having discovered the stone in the dragon's hoard, Bilbo had at first determined with fear and trembling to keep it as his rightful share of the treasure. But things had changed since then. Sick and weary of adventures, he now felt that he would trade this precious prize and more for a chance of seeing the Shire again. Surely Thorin would not let the Arkenstone go unredeemed!

"Why do you come to us?" asked Bard, peering at him sternly across the fire. "Are you a traitor? Do you have tricks up your sleeve?"

Bilbo laughed. "You don't know hobbits, my friend! Believe me, I'm only trying to save us all a lot of trouble."

Bard cocked an eyebrow at the hobbit. "What's in it for you?"

"Bacon and eggs," said Bilbo, smiling. "And a pipe by the fire."

"We have no time for riddles," said the Elvenking. "Speak plainly!"

"Of course!" said Bilbo, drawing the little bundle from his pocket. "I'll be as plain and as brief as possible. I've come to make an offer, you see. Something in the way of a bargaining chip." With a flourish he flung the rags aside and held the gem up before them, a globe of flashing color in the firelight.

Bard blinked and swallowed. The Elvenking rose from his seat and stared down at the shimmering object.

"It's the Arkenstone," said Bilbo in answer to Bard's stunned and questioning look. "The Heart of the Mountain. I feel certain that Thorin Oakenshield will do anything to regain it. Anything you ask."

Then, his head swimming with images of the bright, beautiful, and lovely things that had enticed him to leave his home, Bilbo stretched out his arm and placed the great jewel in Bard's open hand. He bit his lip as the man's fingers closed around it.

"I give it to you," he said, trembling. "May it aid you in your bargaining."

* * * * *

Once upon a time, something happened to someone, and he decided that he would pursue a goal. So he devised a plan of action, and even though there were forces trying to stop him, he moved forward because there was a lot at stake. And just as things seemed as bad as they could get, he learned an

important lesson, and when offered the prize he had
sought so strenuously, he had to decide whether or
not to take it.[72]

This is how writing instructors Gary Provost and Peter
Rubie sum up what they call "the plot for 90 percent of the
stories you've ever read." You can probably see at once how
closely their pattern matches the outline of Bilbo's tale.
One of the most significant points of correspondence,
however, comes in the last sentence: "When offered the
prize he had sought so strenuously, he had to decide
whether or not to take it."

Just for a moment, cast your mind back to the opening
chapter of *The Hobbit*. Do you recall what it was that woke the
"Tookishness" in Bilbo and compelled him to go a-roaming
in the first place? In the final analysis, it was neither altruism,
nor wanderlust, nor secret longings for adventure that convinced him to forsake his armchair and risk the dangers of
the road. Instead, it was the "love of beautiful things made
by hands and by cunning"—the hope of returning with a
share of this gleaming treasure—that motivated him to brave
the perils of mountains, forests, and fire-breathing dragons.

Now redirect your attention to the scene here under consideration. Bilbo, shivering with cold and anticipation, sits in
the camp of the elves and the Lake-men, holding in his hand
the very thing he has crossed the howling wilderness to find:

one of the loveliest and most enchanting treasures ever fashioned "by hands and by cunning"—the Arkenstone of Thrain itself. And he has come to *give it up*. To *hand it over*. To *surrender it* as an act of his own free will. Bilbo, having been "offered the prize he had sought so strenuously" has decided "not to take it." He has learned the important lesson that sacrifice in the cause of the greater good *must* take precedence over personal goals and desires. I don't think it would be going too far to suggest that this moment of choice is *the* conclusive point of the entire drama.

But perhaps it's something more as well. Perhaps Tolkien had a deeper reason, whether conscious or unconscious, for devising this particular climax for his narrative, just as Provost and Rubie had a deeper reason for suggesting that such turnabouts are essential to *all* good storytelling. Perhaps we, the readers, feel the weight of Bilbo's decision all the more forcefully because we understand that learning to *hand it over* is central to the meaning of the human experience. Somewhere deep down inside, we realize that our lives in this world are fleeting and that it is folly to cling to any temporal thing. As a result, though we may not be able to put the thought into words, we sense that surrender is somehow the door to eternity—that a yielding spirit is the key to a vibrant relationship with the living God.

It's impossible not to think of Abraham in this connection. Abraham and Sarah, advanced in age and past all natural hope of begetting and bearing children, longed desperately for a son to inherit the covenant and fulfill the promise they had received from God. When the boy was born, it was as if a miraculous light had dawned upon the old couple. Isaac was not merely the embodiment of their personal hopes and dreams. He was the incarnation of a mind-expanding possibility: the possibility that Abraham's descendants might become "a great nation" someday (Genesis 12:2). And yet no sooner had the patriarch laid hold of this strenuously sought and irreplaceable prize than God asked him to *hand it over*:

Then He said, "Take now your son, your only son Isaac, whom you love, and go to the land of Moriah, and offer him there as a burnt offering on one of the mountains of which I shall tell you." (Genesis 22:2)

In the end, of course, Abraham was not really asked to make this terrible sacrifice. He *was*, however, required to find within himself the *willingness* to make it. It was this openness and willingness that sealed his bond with the invisible and mysterious Author of life, the Source of all blessings and the Giver of all good gifts. "Now I know," said the Lord, "that you fear God, since you have not withheld your son, your only son, from Me" (Genesis 22:12).

Abraham, like Bilbo, had to be ready to surrender his treasure into the hands of Someone capable of putting it to a better and wiser use. And like Christ, he had to learn to hand himself over "to Him who judges justly" (1 Peter 2:23).[73]

Like the apostle Paul, whose human credentials and achievements were the envy of every pious Jew, Abraham was compelled to realize that earth's greatest treasures are nothing but dung in comparison with the higher prize of the "upward call" (Philippians 3:14). Ultimately, it was this realization that made him the "friend of God" (James 2:23) and the "father of many nations" (Genesis 17:5).

"He is no fool who gives what he cannot keep," writes Jim Elliot, "to gain that which he cannot lose."[74] This, in a sense, is the lesson Bilbo learned at the Lonely Mountain. It's also the heart and soul of Christian discipleship—the paradox that underlies the entire economy of Christ's heavenly Kingdom. For as Jesus Himself told us time and time again, it is in yielding that we receive, it is in surrendering that we triumph, and it is in dying that we rise again to eternal life.

REFLECTION
Let go, let God, and live.

THE REAL ENEMY

Bilbo sighed, his breath escaping in a thin white plume. The thing he had dreaded most—the thing he had risked his neck and forfeited his share of the treasure to stave off—was approaching. Up the dale it came in an inexorable gray column: Dain the son of Nain, marching to the aid of his cousin Thorin Oakenshield with five hundred heavily armed dwarves. From where he stood among the Lake-men and the Wood-elves, Bilbo could see their iron caps and mail coats glinting dully in the muffled morning light. Battle, it seemed, was imminent. His bold attempt to force negotiations had failed.

Adventures are not all they're trumped up to be! he thought bitterly. How in the world had his long, eventful journey come to such a senseless end? The dragon was dead, the hoard recovered, and the mountain hall reclaimed. By this time he should have been halfway home, his saddlebags bursting with gold. Instead? Greed. Jealousy. Strife. And now, on top of the rest, open war. Why couldn't Thorin and his thick-headed kin have found a way to make terms with Bard and the Elvenking?

"Dwarves!" grumbled an elvish bowman on the far side of the left flank. "Stubborn, stiff-necked, grasping folk!"

"Aye," muttered one of the Lake-men, somewhere closer at hand. "Though elves like their gems and jewels too, I guess!"

"*And* their river-tolls!" added one of his companions under his breath.

Bilbo's heart sank. So little love lost, even among friends and allies! He'd been noticing it ever since arriving in Bard's camp: men suspicious of elves, elves taking a condescending tone with men. And now it was elves and men together against the dwarves! The hobbit shook his head and adjusted his oversize helmet. Then he gripped his sword and braced himself for the inevitable.

It wasn't long in coming. *Whizz!* A volley of arrows flashed down from the Front Gate of the hall—Thorin and Company getting off the first shot. *Whirr!* Bard's archers turned and responded in kind. At once the narrow strip of land between the spur of the mountain and the loop of the river exploded into a scene of confusion. Shouts rang out in the frosty air. The bowmen of Mirkwood, grim-faced and steel-eyed, dropped to their knees and trained their weapons upon the advancing foe. The dwarves, now no more than fifty yards off, lowered their mattocks and charged. Bard lifted his sword and urged his men forward. Another flight of arrows rained down from the Gate. And then, all in a moment, everything changed.

A clap of thunder split the rocks. The wind surged up, and a pall of darkness fell from the sky like a hammer blow. Every eye turned upward as a vast horde of bats came sweeping down from the north like a cloud of black death. Fell voices howled above the gathering tempest.

"Stop!" cried Gandalf, his voice rebounding off the mountainside. "Leave off your bickering! The goblins are upon us! To me, elves and men and dwarves!"

* * * * *

Spiritual warfare. It's a subject that seems to come up with increasing frequency in these turbulent and troubled times—as well it might. For even under the most benign and benevolent of outward circumstances, the Christian life can always be described as a battle. And the Bible tells us that it is a struggle of *cosmic* significance with *eternal* consequences. No wonder we're exhorted to prepare for the conflict by "tak[ing] up the whole armor of God" (Ephesians 6:13).

FINDING GOD in THE HOBBIT

But before we start sharpening our swords and buckling our breastplates, it might be a good idea to stop and ask a rather basic question: Exactly *who* is the enemy?

There was no confusion on that point among the men, elves, and dwarves who, on the morning of the Battle of Five Armies, found themselves embroiled in a dispute about dragon-gold. It wasn't the first time these groups had clashed. The dwarves and the elves had never been on friendly terms. The elves and men, while generally amiable, had periodic tiffs over tariffs. *Everyone* was smarting under the fallout of Thorin's ill-fated treasure hunt, which had ended in the destruction of Lake-town and the disruption of the river-trade. But while each party had "issues" with the others, all had the sense to lay them aside when the *real* enemy arrived on the scene. As Tolkien explains, "The Goblins were the foes of all, and at their coming all other quarrels were forgotten."[75]

Are we as perceptive as they? Can we tell the difference between a true adversary and an annoying ally? a dangerous opponent and the nuisance next door? To speak more plainly, do we understand that in the fight for God's Kingdom we are *not* making war upon our fellow human beings?

"If only there were evil people somewhere insidiously committing evil deeds," writes author Aleksandr Solzhenitsyn, "and it were necessary only to separate them from the rest of us and destroy them!" His words strike a little too close to home; because if we're honest, we'll have to admit that each of us faces a subtle and perennial temptation to define our spiritual warfare in precisely these terms.

The wise among us know that it can never be that simple. For as Solzhenitsyn goes on to say, "The line dividing good and evil cuts through the heart of every human being."[76] Make no mistake about it. We will never recognize the real Enemy until we realize that the battle is *not* against other people—that it's *not* about the liberals or the conservatives, the homosexuals or the hate mongers, the Republicans or the Democrats, the terrorists, the tyrants, or the cultists.

But while our struggle is not against other mortals, neither does it have much to do with invisible spiritual bogeys. The demonic world is real enough, to be sure, and the supernatural influence of powers and principalities needs to be regarded very seriously (see Ephesians 6:12). But few of us will ever have occasion to wrestle with incarnate fiends (like St. Anthony, the early Desert Father whose biographer recounted several ways in which he was tormented by Satan) or to drive the devil away with a well-aimed ink bottle (like Martin Luther, who hurled the bottle at his unseen enemy one day while translating the Bible into German). For the average believer, the assault is far more subtle.

Who, then, is the real Enemy, and where, in *practical* terms, does the spiritual battlefield lie? The Bible tells us in no uncertain terms:

Beloved, I beg you as sojourners and pilgrims, abstain from fleshly lusts which war against the soul. (1 Peter 2:11)

The flesh lusts against the Spirit, and the Spirit against the flesh; and these are contrary to one another, so that you do not do the things that you wish. (Galatians 5:17)

I find then a law, that evil is present with me, the one who wills to do good. For I delight in the law of God according to the inward man. But I see another law in my members, warring against the law of my mind, and bringing me into captivity to the law of sin which is in my members. (Romans 7:21-23)

To put it another way, the most formidable opponent you will ever face in the fight for the Kingdom is . . . *yourself.* The toughest battle you will ever endure is the one that gets played out on the field of *self*-discipline, *self*-control, and moment-by-moment reliance upon the indwelling presence of God. It's an *inward*, not an *outward* struggle. But fierce as it is, the battle is not hopeless. On the contrary, Paul tells us that it is being won every day. "Walk in the Spirit," he exhorts us, "and you shall not fulfill the lust of the flesh" (Galatians 5:16). *That's* what spiritual warfare is all about.

Christians through the ages have understood this and ordered their lives accordingly. They have seen clearly, as Pascal says, "that man has no other enemy but concupiscence, which turns him away from God, and not [human] enemies."[77] So firmly did the monks of the ancient Celtic tradition believe this that they devoted every inch of their being and every ounce of their strength to the task of combating this foe. Faustus of Riez, an abbot of the fifth century, expresses it this way:

> It is not for quiet and security . . . that we have formed a community in the monastery, but for a struggle and a conflict. We have met here for a contest, we have embarked upon a war against our sins. . . . We have gathered together in this tranquil retreat, this spiritual camp, that we may day after day wage an unwearying war against our passions.[78]

May we find the courage and the determination to do the same.

REFLECTION

"We have met the enemy, and he is us."[79]

RECURRING SHADOWS

It was late, and Bilbo was struggling against the soporific effects of the ale and the music. Up the walls and through the rafters flew the rippling notes of the elven harps, chasing one another from beam to beam like sporting birds in a lofty green wood. Around and around in the hobbit's brain spun the tail end of the elven song, drifting and eddying like a skittering pinwheel of dry leaves in a spiraling breeze:

Come! Tra-la-la-lally!
Come back to the valley!

The hobbit unbuttoned his waistcoat, interlaced his fingers over his belt, and smiled. His eyelids drooped. *There is nothing,* he thought, *like dinner in the house of Elrond. Dinner followed by a round of songs and tales!* Slowly the hall began to fade around him. . . .

"And thus it happened," he heard Gandalf say just as he was about to drop off, "that Saruman agreed at last to make an assault against the Necromancer."

One of Bilbo's eyes popped open. He sat up and cocked an ear in the wizard's direction.

"Against Dol Guldur itself?" said Master Elrond, raising an eyebrow. "I see. It has been a long time coming."

"Yes," sighed Gandalf. "Ninety-one years since first I urged it upon the Council. Ninety-one years since I entered that terrible place and found Thorin's father, Thrain, gibbering in the pits. He died there, as you know. I myself barely escaped. But my suspicions were confirmed. I knew then beyond a doubt that the Shadow had risen again."

"As so many times before. But was the plan carried out?"

"Oh, yes." The wizard put his fingertips together, sat back in his great carved chair, and shut his eyes. "Yes, indeed."

"And?" Elrond, like Bilbo, leaned forward in his seat.

Gandalf laughed softly. "It was all too easy! A token resistance. None lost on our side. A few on theirs. Before long he turned and fled. Simply vanished. But I fear it was a mere feint. My heart tells me his plans had long been laid."

"Then you believe he has gone to——"

"Can there be any question about it?"

Bilbo saw Master Elrond shake his head. A long silence followed.

"But we mustn't look so glum!" said Gandalf, suddenly brightening, his blue eyes sparkling beneath his bristling brows. "A great evil has departed from the North! That in itself is cause for rejoicing. Though I wish he were gone for good."

Master Elrond smiled grimly. "Unlikely in this age of the world," he observed. "Though it is always good to hope."

Bilbo shivered slightly before closing his eyes and sinking back in his chair again.

* * * * *

The Hobbit was a virtual overnight success upon its initial release in 1937. Demands for a sequel followed almost immediately. Enthusiastic fans were eager to learn more about Gondolin and the House of Elrond. Others craved accounts of dwarvish history or detailed descriptions of the Shire and its surroundings. Young Priscilla Tolkien told her father that she was looking forward to getting better acquainted with the eccentric Took family.[80] The publishers, Allen & Unwin, had visions of expanding their profits.

But perhaps the keenest expressions of interest came from readers who wanted to know more about the *Necromancer*.[81] Indeed, it was partly in response to persistent inquiries on this theme that Tolkien gave the Black Sorcerer of Dol Guldur such a pivotal role in the books that were to follow; so that this shadowy, indistinct figure was revealed to be none other than Sauron, ruler of Mordor and master of Barad-dûr—the terrible Lord of the Rings himself.

Remarkable, isn't it? So much attention is focused on a marginal character of (apparently) incidental significance. But then perhaps this isn't so surprising. After all, everybody loves a good villain. And not without good reason. For the heart and soul of effective drama is *conflict*.

"It is a strange thing," says Tolkien in chapter 3 of *The Hobbit*, "but things that are good to have and days that are good to spend are soon told about, and not much to listen to; while things that are uncomfortable, palpitating, and even gruesome, may make a good tale."[82] A truer word was never spoken—true in real life as well as in the world of entertainment.

It's also true, I believe, in the realm of the spirit. As it turns out, the sparks generated by the friction of adversity are more than just the stuff of engaging fiction. They're also the fuel of a vibrant, vital, vertically oriented life. Oddly enough, the God-directed inner self seems to *require* conflict for the development of a keen spiritual edge. Somehow or other, the tender plant of the soul appears to thrive best under the threat of a shadow.

It's no coincidence that David fell prey to temptation at a

time when he *should* have been in harm's way at the head of his army (2 Samuel 11:1). Nor is it surprising that deliverance from foes and periods of ease and rest so often produced indolence and apostasy in the life of ancient Israel. "Before I was afflicted I went astray," writes the psalmist, "But now I keep Your word" (Psalm 119:67). Apparently we *need* an element of darkness and danger in our lives to keep us on the straight and narrow.

The good news, I suppose, is that this element will never be far to seek so long as we live in this world. For however valiantly it may be opposed, however thoroughly it may be beaten, however soundly it may be drummed off the stage of history, the shadow of evil always rises again.

Gandalf and Master Elrond understood this. They realized that the Necromancer was no newcomer to the lands of Middle-earth. They knew that they had encountered this enemy before. In long ages past, this same Sauron had been cowed by the Númenóreans, thwarted and exiled by the Valar, destroyed in battle by Isildur. His insidious devices had been challenged, confronted, and defeated time and time again. And yet in every case he had managed to reappear, in another age, another place, another face. Now the drama was being played out again: After more than eighteen centuries of watching Sauron's power grow, the White Council had succeeded at last in driving him from his latest stronghold—the tower of Dol Guldur in the southern marches of Mirkwood. But the Wise knew that they had not seen the end of this deadly foe.

What the Wise knew we must also learn and continually bear in mind. For in spite of the myths of evolution, civilization, and social progress, evil is always lurking somewhere just beyond the range of the light. Pending the ultimate renewal of creation, it is constantly crouching at the door, rearing its head in some new and different guise. Banished from heaven (Revelation 12:9), the great red dragon quickly reestablishes himself upon the earth (Revelation 12:13). And he is subtle enough to assume the appearance of an angel of light (2 Corinthians 11:14).

This is the insight that struck Tolkien so forcibly when, in the wake of the success of his *Hobbit* "sequel," he contemplated the possibility of taking up his pen once more, this time to record the history of Middle-earth as it might have unfolded in the years following the events of *The Lord of the Rings*:

[I once wrote] the beginning of a tale supposed to refer to the end of the reign of Eldaron about 100 years after the death of Aragorn. Then I of course discovered that the King's Peace would contain no tales worth recounting; and his wars would have little interest after the overthrow of Sauron; but that almost certainly a restlessness would appear about then, owing to the (it seems) inevitable boredom of Men with the good.[83]

Like it or not, this is the way of the world. The Necromancer, once defeated, resurfaces as the Lord of Mordor. And if by some miracle the Lord of Mordor should be utterly destroyed at last, all that's needed to fill his place is the "boredom of Men with the good."

So be sober and vigilant. Remember that "your adversary the devil walks about like a roaring lion, seeking whom he may devour." He will never be completely banished until this age of the world comes to an end. But he *can* be effectively resisted in the here and now—*if* we will remain "steadfast in the faith" (I Peter 5:8-9).

REFLECTION

While the world endures, the fight continues.

*He was quite content; and the
sound of the kettle on his hearth
was ever after more musical than
it had been even in the quiet days
before the Unexpected Party.*

—*THE HOBBIT*, CHAPTER 19,
"THE LAST STAGE"

"... AND BACK
AGAIN"

Bilbo's heart was thumping with excitement. How often in
the course of the past year had he dreamed of this moment?
It was impossible to say; and yet he remembered clearly that
at almost every turn—beneath the Misty Mountains or in
the dark forest of Mirkwood; riddling with Gollum or feasting in Beorn's hall; in battles with spiders, visits with elves,
barrel rides on the river, or conversations with the dragon—
wherever he had gone and whatever he had been doing, his
thoughts had always returned to his comfortable hobbit-
hole under the Hill. How many times had he pined for his
armchair and his cup! How keenly had he longed to hear the

sweet sound of the kettle singing on the hearth! And now at last the goal was within sight.

The top of the Hill rose from behind an intervening ridge as he and Gandalf rounded the last bend. Bilbo drew his pipe and leaf-pouch from his pocket, savoring the thought of a leisurely smoke beside the round green door. But as the garden gate came into view, he suddenly dropped both pipe and pouch and nearly sat down in the road from shock.

"Well!" said Gandalf, stroking his beard. "It seems I spoke true when I warned of a long road ahead!"

Bilbo nodded and stared in disbelief. His garden was full of Shire-folk. Hobbits here and hobbits there, hobbits trampling the flower beds, talking animatedly, milling about the door. In their midst, atop the bench where Bilbo used to sit and blow smoke-rings, stood his cousins Otho and Lobelia Sackville-Baggins, presiding over a heap of boxes and bags and an assortment of sofas, settles, and sideboards—Bilbo's furniture! It all looked strangely faded and threadbare in the late morning sun. Otho kept shouting things like, "Five! I have five!" and "Who shall make it five-and-quarter?" On the gate hung a sign in black and red:

AUCTION: ESTATE OF THE LATE MR. BILBO BAGGINS. SALE COMMENCING AT TEN O' CLOCK.

Bilbo groaned.

In the end, it required a good bit of dragon-gold to convince Otho and Lobelia that the rumors of Bilbo's death had been greatly exaggerated. That's not to mention the money he had to spend buying back the items sold prior to his arrival. But that was a matter of small consequence. At this point the main thing was to regain his home and reclaim his place by the hearth—at *any* cost.

That evening, as he and the wizard sat together in the parlor stirring their tea and spreading marmalade on their toast, Bilbo couldn't help but recall a snatch of song he'd heard the elves singing in Rivendell:

> *The fire is more shining*
> *On hearth in the gloaming*
> *Than gold won by mining,*
> *So why go a-roaming?*

Why indeed? He smiled and passed the sugar bowl to Gandalf.

"One lump or two?"

* * * * *

My friend and writing partner Kurt Bruner has on several occasions done me the singular honor of calling me a hobbit. I have a feeling he doesn't know the half of it.

As a rule, hobbits don't care for adventures. As a rule, neither do I. Hobbits, for the most part, tend to be stay-at-homes: provincials with little or no interest in rambles and travels and a strong taste for the plain and simple pleasures of table and garden and hearth. Ditto here. Wealth and status hold no enticements for them; they prefer a steaming cup and a good book by the fire. Even more to the point, they regard people who crave a challenge—the kind who climb rocks or run marathons or jockey for positions of corporate authority—as a little bit "touched" or "cracked." My feelings exactly.

Not that I haven't had my share of adventures. Relatively tame and inconsequential ones of course. Nothing like the dangers Bilbo Baggins had to face. Entirely unworthy of comparison with the life experiences of most of my readers, I'm sure. But I *have* landed myself in a few tight spots and wormed my way out of several touch-and-go situations. I've been shoved out of my comfort zone and forced to take on stretching assignments. I've done things I didn't think I was capable of doing—like passing algebra, or raising six kids, or writing this book. Life has a way of doing that to you: It pushes you beyond the borders of your personal Shire and compels you to engage the wider world. Whether you like it or not.

And yet, when all's been said and done, adventures and challenges are *not* what life is all about. Exciting, stimulating, and character-building though they may be, excursions into the wild beyond are really just episodic intrusions into the long-range business of existence. The bigger issue is finding fulfillment back at the place where it all began. In other words, it's a question of *contentment*. A matter of *coming home*. At least that's how I see it.

For all the "Tookishness" he'd inherited on his mother's side, Bilbo seems to have felt the same way. Yes, he heard the call of the wild. Not only did he hear, he followed. With Gandalf and Thorin and twelve stout dwarves, he crossed the known world in search of mountains, lakes, dragons, and treasures. He sojourned with elves, encountered the power of enchantments, and viewed wonders beyond the comprehension of any other living hobbit. But in his heart, however dire the dilemma, however hot the fight, however stirring the struggle, Bilbo could never quite forget his snug little home under the Hill in Hobbiton. Memories of its quiet joys and humble pleasures thrust themselves into his conscious thoughts at almost every turn in the road. Not until he had reached his own doorstep did he consider the tale of his daring journey complete.

It's not to cast blame on Bilbo or to impugn his character that the narrator tells us this. On the contrary, these insights into the inner workings of the hobbit's mind are related with tenderness and empathy. To a great extent, they reflect Tolkien's personal perspective. As he once told an inquirer,

"I am in fact a *Hobbit* (in all but size)."[84] And what better place for a hobbit than at home in his armchair with the kettle boiling and the lamp shining?

Charles Williams, publisher, author, and member of the Inklings, seems to have appreciated this aspect of his friend's writings. "C. Williams," writes Tolkien, "who is reading it all [i.e., *The Lord of the Rings*] says the great thing is that its *centre* is not in strife and war and heroism (though they are understood and depicted) but in freedom, peace, ordinary life and good liking."[85]

Ordinary life and good liking. These are the things that hobbits treasure most. That's why Bilbo, at the end of his road, was willing to pay any price, up to and including heaps of hard-won dwarvish gold, to regain the simple prize of hearth and home. If I may be so bold as to say it, I believe this is the very thing that makes him a role model worthy of our emulation. Even crusty old Thorin Oakenshield came to see this before the end. "There is more in you of good than you know," said the dying Thorin to Bilbo. "If more of us valued food and cheer and song above hoarded gold, it would be a merrier world."[86]

A merrier world indeed. A world, in fact, such as God intends the world to be: a place where the simple joys of the Shire-folk reign supreme and where the redeemed know beyond a shadow of a doubt that "godliness with contentment" is the greatest gain of all (I Timothy 6:6).

In that blessed land,

> *They shall beat their swords into plowshares,*
> *And their spears into pruning hooks;*
> *Nation shall not lift up sword against nation,*
> *Neither shall they learn war anymore.*
> *But everyone shall sit under his vine and under his fig tree,*
> *And no one shall make them afraid. (Micah 4:3-4)*[87]

Do you remember how the great epic of *The Lord of the Rings* ends? It comes back to the place where Bilbo's adventures began: all the way back to Bag-End, where Rosie waits for Sam on the doorstep, and where there is a fire on the hearth, and yellow light within, and dinner on the table:

And Rose drew him in, and set him in his chair, and put little Elanor upon his lap.

He drew a deep breath. "Well, I'm back," he said.[88]

REFLECTION
Contentment is wealth.

"Surely you don't disbelieve the prophecies, because you had a hand in bringing them about yourself? You don't really suppose, do you, that all your adventures and escapes were managed by mere luck, just for your sole benefit?"

—THE HOBBIT, CHAPTER 19,
"THE LAST STAGE"

WHO WOVE THE WEB?

Adventures, as Bilbo discovered, though uncomfortable and bothersome to have, can be extremely pleasant to remember. It is an odd but noteworthy fact that the delight of recalling dangerous scrapes and narrow escapes increases steadily with the passage of the years. Pleasantest of all, perhaps, is the prospect of writing them out on great sheets of paper in a broad, flowing hand while seated in front of a crackling fire on a chilly autumn evening—as the hobbit was doing when someone rang the bell.

"Gandalf!" he cried, opening the door and nearly jumping with surprise. "My dear Gandalf! What a long time it's been! And Balin! How your beard has grown!"

"As has the expanse of your waistcoat, my fine hobbit!" said the dwarf, laughing.

It was only natural that they should spend the rest of the evening talking over old times. Bilbo produced cakes and ale and a seasoned ham, and when they had finished eating, they heaped up the fire, lit their pipes, and went on reminiscing far into the night.

"What a scene we must have made when we arrived in Lake-town!" said Bilbo, sending up a small cloud of smoke toward the ceiling. "All bedraggled and rumpled and dripping. And you dwarves with bits of sawdust and twigs in your beards!"

"I'll never forget it!" said a frowning Balin, puffing out a series of concentric smoke rings. "Nor the look on the Master's face when we walked into his hall. It's a wonder we weren't sent packing at once!"

Gandalf closed his eyes and blew out a flock of six smoky geese. Straight as six arrows they flew through Balin's rings and disappeared into Bilbo's cloud. "An odd character," said the wizard thoughtfully. "The Master, I mean."

"A shrewd fellow, I thought," said Bilbo. "What's become of him? Did he rebuild Esgaroth with the gold Bard gave him?"

"Not he!" said Gandalf, scowling. "He took that treasure and fled with it. To his own demise. No, it's his successor, the new Master, who has put things back on a solid footing in Lake-town. A pity the old one never got to see the prophecies fulfilled."

Bilbo looked at him curiously. "Prophecies?"

"Rivers of gold!" said Balin with a wink. "Trade on the river is livelier than ever now that old Smaug's gone. Lake-town has never been so prosperous!"

Bilbo set his pipe on the fender and leaned back in his chair. "So it's all come true in a way," he said wonderingly. "The return of the King under the Mountain. Wealth flowing in fountains. Streams burning with gladness. And to think that *I* had a hand in bringing it about!"

Gandalf opened one eye and smiled at him. "You needn't burst any of those gold buttons," he said. "Haven't I told you before that there is more than one power at work in this world? And more threads in the web of stories than you dream of! Believe me, Mr. Baggins, you are only a very little fellow after all!"

* * * * *

And so we come at last to the end of the story of Bilbo Baggins, hobbit of the Shire, a small and ordinary person caught up in a web of great and momentous events. It's a remarkable tale for a number of memorable reasons. But perhaps the most remarkable and memorable thing about it is the light it sheds on the stories of so many *other* small and insignificant people—people like you and me.

Why do I say this? Because Bilbo, despite his diminutive size and apparent unimportance, ends up impacting his world in ways he is incapable of comprehending. He finds a Ring that eventually procures the downfall of a Shadow. He spares a life and ensures the salvation of the world. He influences the outcome of battles and paves the way for the fulfillment of age-old prophecies. He accomplishes most of these things without knowing exactly what he is doing or why. In the upshot, his life becomes a crucial brushstroke in the scheme of a much bigger picture—an indispensable thread in a tapestry of grand and far-reaching design.

That tapestry is the theme of "The Quest of Erebor," a "deleted scene" from *The Lord of the Rings* in which Tolkien records a conversation that takes place between Gandalf, Frodo, Merry, Pippin, and Gimli at the conclusion of the epic adventure. Gimli, marveling at the string of interconnected events that had led them to this moment of new beginnings, expresses a desire to see the Shire, home of the humble hobbits. "Did not the recovery of the Kingship under the Mountain, and the fall of Smaug, begin there?" he says. "Not to mention the end of Barad-dûr, though both were strangely woven together."

Strangely woven indeed. But "strange" is not the final

word here. For it's precisely at this point that Gimli turns to Gandalf and asks the million-dollar question—the question we hinted at in our reflection on Bilbo's riddle game with Gollum. "Who wove the web?" he wants to know. "Did you plan all this then, Gandalf?"

Gandalf's answer is telling:

> I do not know the answer. . . . But such measures are meaningless. In that far distant time I said to a small and frightened hobbit: Bilbo was *meant* to find the Ring, and *not* by its maker, and you [Frodo] therefore were *meant* to bear it. And I might have added: and I was *meant* to guide you both to those points.[89]

Herein, I think, lies the key to the deeper significance of the hobbit's story. For if Bilbo was *meant* to find and Frodo was *meant* to bear—if indeed even Gandalf himself was *meant* to guide—then *Someone else* must have been in the wings contriving all this "meaning."

Who was that Someone? Who but the Master Weaver? Who but the "Writer of the Story" (by which I do *not* mean Tolkien)?[90] Who but the "one ever-present Person who is never absent and never named"[91] throughout all the vast web of tales that span the history of the peoples of Middle-earth?

Late in life Tolkien had an experience that brought this concept home to him in a profoundly personal way. He was visited in Oxford by a man who "had been much struck by the curious way in which many old pictures seemed to him to have been designed to illustrate *The Lord of the Rings* long before its time." The visitor produced copies of these paintings and asked Tolkien if they had influenced his storytelling in any way. Oddly enough, the aging author responded that he had never seen them before. At this the man fell strangely silent.

"I became aware that he was looking fixedly at me," writes Tolkien. "Suddenly he said: 'Of course you don't suppose, do you, that you wrote all that book yourself?'"

Tolkien continues: "Pure Gandalf! . . . I think I said: 'No, I don't suppose so any longer.' I have never since been able to suppose so. An alarming conclusion for an old philologist to draw concerning his private amusement."[92]

There's an application here for each and every one of us. Like Bilbo, Frodo, Gandalf, and J. R. R. Tolkien himself, we are all players in a drama far greater in scope and more all-encompassing in its implications than anything we are capable of grasping. Like Joseph, who told his brothers, "You meant evil against me; but God meant it for good" (Genesis 50:20), we can know that whatever happens to us, however we trip or fumble or fall, there is another Power operating behind the scenes. We do not think or act or speak alone. Even our "private amusements" are not our own. There *is* a method to the madness. There *is* an "Intelligent Design." *Someone else* is writing the script and calling the shots.

Christians have the privilege of knowing that ever-present

Person's name. It is *Jesus*. *He* is the Weaver of the Web and the Writer of the Tale: the Alpha and the Omega, the Living Word incarnate, the One through whom all things were made and in whom all things hold together (John 1:3; Colossians 1:15-18). It is in *Him*, as the apostle Paul told the Athenians on Mars Hill, that "we live and move and have our being" (Acts 17:28). "For of Him and through Him and to Him are all things, to whom be glory forever. Amen" (Romans 11:36).

I don't think there can be a better place to conclude our tour of the tale of Mr. Baggins. For in the end, it's only in the assurance of this grand and all-encompassing message that we, like Bilbo himself, may set forth with full confidence upon the road to high adventure.

REFLECTION

"The Writer of the Story is not one of us."[93]

Afterthoughts

All this happened a long time ago: It was summer, and I had been reading Mark Twain's *Tom Sawyer* for the first time. I couldn't have been more than eleven or twelve years old. Yet I can picture the whole thing as if it were yesterday.

Two-thirty in the morning. The house dark and silent. My parents, my sister, my little brother, all asleep in their beds. And me, in bathrobe and slippers, rummaging a candle—one of the dirty white stumps my mom keeps around the house in case of power outages—from a kitchen drawer.

A flicker of blue. Sudden shadows leap against the wall as I light my candle at the stove burner. I cast a disdainful backward glance at the flashlight where it lies forsaken at the bottom of the drawer. Tom Sawyer wouldn't have used a flashlight.

With bated breath, I proceed on tiptoe to the back door. Bending to my task like one trying to crack a safe, I twist the knob and press my body against the lock to muffle the inevitable *click*. The door swings inward. There is a rush of cool air against my face. Candle at arm's length, pale yellow flame fluttering tenuously in the night breeze, I step out under the stars. The grass is wet with dew, and the dampness soon seeps through the papery soles of my slippers. I shiver involuntarily and head off down the street.

Before my mind's eye shimmers a clear image: a gaggle of ramshackle sheds and huts huddled together down by the railroad tracks—a veritable hobo's shanty, not more than a mile from my house. Bums live down there, they say. Tramps and rail riders. I have visited the place once or twice, with friends in the daylight. I've seen the evidence. Cans and bottles. Rusty bedsprings and shredded mattresses. Scraps of old clothes.

The spark of my candle winks in the windows of the watchful houses. Treading softly, I shut my eyes and conjure up a vision of hungry, hard-faced men stooping over a campfire, sipping black coffee from tin cans. They have grizzled chins and dirty black hats, and they carry bundles in red bandanas at the ends of crooked sticks. I'm determined to go and see them for myself. In the middle of the night. With a candle. Because that's the sort of thing Tom Sawyer would do.

I suppose it would be a good idea to stop here and issue a

disclaimer: *Kids, don't try this at home.* Instead, tremble at the appalling spectacle of my boyish naïveté. Remember this was, after all, Los Angeles, not Hannibal. Who knows what I, a mere tender child, might have stumbled upon in those derelict shacks by the railroad tracks at two-thirty in the morning? It's a disconcerting thought.

Luckily for me, I never made it that far. As a matter of fact, I never got past my friend Jeff's house, two doors down the block. To my dismay, Jeff *wasn't* waiting for me when, according to plan, I came up under his bedroom window and mewed like a cat. I mewed and mewed again, but the slacker never showed. Eventually I was forced to abort the mission, snuff out my candle, and go on back to bed.

I guess Jeff hadn't read *Tom Sawyer.*

Living the Story

The point of this little vignette should be obvious. *Story* has always exerted a tremendous power over me. As a boy, I regarded reading as serious business. When I found a tale I liked, I did more than devour it—I tried to *live* it. Like Tom Sawyer himself, the Missouri boy who "ambuscaded A-rabs" and turned Jackson's Island into a private Sherwood Forest, I patterned my day-to-day existence after the adventures of my literary heroes. I did everything by the book. Straw hat. Bare feet. Even the inevitable (though unsmokable) corncob pipe.

The remarkable thing is that it was in much the same way that I eventually came to know the reality of the living Christ as a high-school student. I was a church kid who had been raised in Sunday school. I knew long passages of the Old and New Testaments by heart. I'd had the benefit of the finest resources and the most dedicated teachers any child could ever hope to have. I'd been through confirmation class, earned my Bible, and officially joined the church. Stacked away in the storeroom of my heart and mind were bundles and bundles of seasoned fuel just waiting to feed the fire that was to come. But the thing that actually ignited the flame and brought the dry bones to life was the power of story: the Greatest Story Ever Told.

My Sunday school teacher that summer was a college student named Rich. Rich didn't go in much for curriculum and lesson plans. He just told the story of Jesus. He took us straight through the book of Mark, starting with "the beginning of the gospel of Jesus Christ" and ending with "they went out and preached everywhere." It was all there, just as I'd heard it so many times before. The calling of the disciples. The walks and talks by the seaside. The healings and the miracles. The agony of the Cross and the glory of the Resurrection.

But somehow in Rich's mouth the whole thing came to life in a brand-new way. Somehow, as he spoke, I could smell the sea of Galilee and hear the Master's voice. I felt what it was like to travel with Him over dusty roads on sweaty, sandaled feet. I experienced the tale as an *adventure*—a quest, a journey, an exciting exploit like Bilbo Baggins's excursion into Wilderland with Gandalf, and Thorin and Company. As I sat there listening, I was struck with a realization that stirred me to the core: *This guy really believes what he's saying.*

I knew Rich believed it because he did more than simply tell the story. He connected it with his own experience. As a member of our church's "Summer Deputation Team," Rich was heavily involved with what came to be known as the Jesus Movement in Southern California. That's how it happened that as we went through the story of Jesus, we also got snatches and snippets of the story of Rich. We learned how he and his teammates spent their days by the seaside, proclaiming the Good News from Huntington to Redondo Beach to Will Rogers State Beach. We followed them into the streets of Hollywood where they labored into the night, talking with hippies and making friends with prostitutes and street people. We heard about the "crash house" ministry and the Salt Company Coffee House and the Bible studies with social dropouts and former dopeheads and runaway kids.

As I listened to Rich describe all of this—as I heard him draw parallels between the events of the Gospel narrative and his own adventures on the beaches and the streets—it suddenly occurred to me what he was doing. He was *living the story*. He was taking the tale out of the book and into the streets. This was something I could understand. This was something I could connect with my own life experience and my own way of approaching the world. And it was this that sparked a fire in my heart, made me *love* the story as never before, and inspired me, like Rich, to *live it* to the best of my poor ability.

Embodying Truth

It's at this point that I'd like to take another look at Tolkien's vigorous protests against the idea that his tales could be interpreted as allegory—protests that *might* be taken to mean that we have no business trying to "find God" in a book like *The Hobbit.*

We know that the professor was quite adamant about this. "There is *no* 'symbolism' or conscious allegory in my story," he declares.[95] In another place he asserts, "I am not naturally attracted (in fact much the reverse) by allegory, mystical or moral."[96]

Yet for all this, Tolkien himself was not above making "allegorical" comparisons between certain elements of his fictional world and the realities of everyday existence. In one of his letters he characterizes the more distasteful aspects of "progressive" modern life as "Mordor in our midst."[97] He describes his son Christopher, on duty with the RAF during the Second World War, as "a hobbit amongst the Urukhai."[98] He sums up his assessment of the war effort by calling it an attempt "to conquer Sauron with the Ring."[99] In short, he sees life through the lens of his story and "interprets" the story in terms of current events.

In making such statements, was the author of *The Hobbit* and *The Lord of the Rings* betraying his own principles? Had he somehow forgotten his disdain for allegory? Was he talking out of two sides of his mouth? Or was he simply engaging in a bit of lighthearted humor at his own expense?

The real explanation, I believe, is that Tolkien understood, as many of his readers and critics did not, that it is one thing to concoct an allegory and quite another to reflect universal principles and eternal realities in a timeless tale. "That there is no allegory does not, of course, say there is no applicability," he writes. "There always is."[100] He even goes so far as to suggest that our finest examples of myth making and fictional art can sometimes achieve a life of their own, a life which manifests itself as a powerful and deeply affecting blend of *both* allegory *and* story: "It is I suppose impossible to write any 'story' that is not allegorical in proportion as it 'comes to life'; since each of us is an allegory, embodying in a particular tale and clothed in the garments of time and place, universal truth and everlasting life."[101]

Each of us is an allegory. I find that to be an extremely uplifting and inspiring thought. Another way to say it is that a well-lived life, like a well-told tale—and vice versa—becomes a kind of *incarnation* of the Truth: a visible, tangible representation of the intentions of the Author of the human story. This, I think, is what Tolkien has in mind when he observes that "the only perfectly consistent allegory is a real life; and the only fully intelligible story is an allegory."[102]

The Bright Shadow

Life as *allegory*. Fiction as *embodiment* and *incarnation*. Story and the daily grind coming together in that "sweet spot" we experience as vibrant light and truth. I couldn't possibly have articulated these ideas when I was eleven years old. And yet, in retrospect, I can't help thinking that they had something to do with the impulse that drove me to act out the things I read in *The Adventures of Tom Sawyer*.

The same impulse stirred in me again when I encountered *The Hobbit* for the first time. It thrust itself upon me with a climactic, consummating, and all-consuming force when, a few months later, I witnessed the story of Jesus brought to life in the example of my eleventh-grade Sunday school teacher. As I set out to follow that example and live that adventure for myself—a process that continues down to this very moment—I began to grasp the essential point: God meets us *not* through concepts, curricula, or catechisms, but in that miraculous place where *the Word becomes Flesh*; the place where we, like the fishermen of Galilee, suddenly find ourselves swept up into the plot of the greatest Story of all.

A similar realization seems to have dawned upon C. S. Lewis on that historic night in 1916 when he picked up a copy of George MacDonald's *Phantastes*. In MacDonald's storytelling Lewis found neither an allegory nor a symbolic representation of the Christian message, but rather a mysteriously compelling *incarnation* of the thing he had been seeking all his life: *joy*. And what surprised him most about his discovery was that this shimmering embodiment of his most deeply felt desires, for all its fantastical fairy-tale trappings, was clearly, unmistakably, and unalterably linked with the humble realities of everyday life:

> But now I saw the bright shadow coming out of the book into the real world and resting there, transforming all common things and yet itself unchanged. Or, more accurately, I saw the common things drawn into the bright shadow. [103]

> The quality which had enchanted me in [MacDonald's] imaginative works turned out to be the quality of the real universe, the divine, magical, terrifying and ecstatic reality in which we all live. [104]

This is what good literature, especially good fantasy literature, is supposed to do for us. I believe it is also a fair description of what *The Hobbit* and the rest of J. R. R. Tolkien's fictional works did for *me* during the seminal stages of my life's journey. Through the ruse of an entertaining and imaginative tale, Tolkien drew back the veil of familiarity and boredom that covered my school-day existence and revealed the world to me in a new light, as a land of perilous beauty and wondrous delight, a place gloriously haunted by the Presence of a Person "who is never absent and never named."

When the "bright shadow" of the shining adventure comes out of the Book and rests upon *your* life, you, too, will know what it means to be irreversibly transformed. In that moment, you will see that, the pros and cons of allegory and symbolism notwithstanding, it *is* possible to *find God* in a book like *The Hobbit*. Most importantly, you will understand that God can and does *find us* almost anywhere—that He seeks us in the most unlikely places and draws us to Himself even when we're not looking for Him.

It's a realization from which there can be no turning back.

Notes

1. Lewis, *Surprised by Joy*, 145.

2. Ibid., 146.

3. Tolkien, *Letters*, no. 328, p. 413.

4. Bruner and Ware, *Finding God in The Lord of the Rings*, xiii.

5. Tolkien, *Letters*, no. 213, p. 288.

6. Ibid., no. 269, p. 355.

7. Ibid., no. 153, p. 194.

8. Lewis, *Of Other Worlds*, 37.

9. Tolkien, *Letters*, no. 310, p. 400.

10. Kilby, *Tolkien and The Silmarillion*, 79.

11. Bruner and Ware, *Finding God in the Land of Narnia*, xviii.

12. Tolkien, *Unfinished Tales*, 337.

13. Tolkien, *Reader*, 47 ff.

14. Tolkien, *Silmarillion*, 43.

15. Tolkien, *Unfinished Tales*, 336.

16. Tolkien, *Hobbit*, 28.

17. Ibid., 22.

18. Bonhoeffer, *Discipleship*, 157–8.

19. Tolstoy, *Christianity and Patriotism*.

20. From "A Mighty Fortress Is Our God."

21. Based on *The Hobbit*, chapter 3: "A Short Rest."

22. Tolkien, *Letters*, no. 35, p. 42.

23. Tolkien, *Hobbit*, 48–9.

24. Tolkien, *Letters*, no. 131, p. 146.

25. Ibid., no. 156, p. 202.

26. Tolkien, *Lord of the Rings*, 348.

27. Tolkien, *Hobbit*, 60.

28. Tolkien, *Letters*, no. 131, pp. 145–6.

29. Tolkien, *Hobbit*, 74.

30. Tolkien, *Unfinished Tales*, 348.

31. Tolkien, *Lord of the Rings*, 73.

32. Tolkien, *Letters*, no. 192, p. 253.

33. Ibid., no. 181, p. 234.

34. Aelfric, *Lives of the Saints*, 2:314–35.

35. J. R. R. Tolkien, C. S. Lewis, and a number of their friends and colleagues formed a group known as the Inklings.

36. Tolkien, *Silmarillion*, 46, 228.

37. Ibid., 25–6.

38. For further illustrations of the special role played by the eagles, see *The Silmarillion*, 110, 182, 277, and *The Hobbit*, chapter 17: "The Clouds Burst."

39. See *The Lord of the Rings*, Book I, chapter 7.

40. Grotta-Kurska, *Architect of Middle-earth*, 19.

41. Carpenter, *Biography*, 139.

42. Tolkien, *Hobbit*, 60.

NOTES

43. Tolkien, *Lord of the Rings*, 494.

44. *The Catechism of the Catholic Church*, section 339.

45. Tolkien, *Letters*, no. 96, p. 110.

46. Joan Whitney and Alex Kramer, "Far Away Places with Strange Sounding Names," 1948; recorded by Bing Crosby, Margaret Whiting, Perry Como, and Dinah Shore.

47. Tolkien, *Letters*, no. 328, p. 412.

48. Ibid., no. 247, p. 333.

49. "Ein begriffener Gott ist kein Gott," Gerhart Tersteegen (1697–69), quoted in Otto, *The Idea of the Holy*, 25.

50. Clement, *Epistle of Clement to James*, chapter 3, in *The Ante-Nicene Fathers*, vol. 8.

51. *New Advent Catholic Encyclopedia*, s.v. "St. Ceadda," www.newadvent.org/cathen/03470c.htm (October 6, 2005).

52. Livy, *The Early History of Rome*, Book 4. Under the constitution of the Roman Republic, consuls had the power to appoint a dictator during times of national crisis. The dictator was granted absolute power for a period of six months.

53. Letter to Tench Coxe, 1799. Cited in *The Oxford Dictionary of Quotations*, 268.

54. Tolkien, *Hobbit*, 189.

55. Mills, "Take Me!"

56. See, e.g., *Letters*, no. 215, p. 297: "When I published *The Hobbit*—hurriedly and without due consideration—I was still influenced by the convention that 'fairy-stories' are naturally directed to children. . . . And I had children of my own." Also no. 257, p. 346: "I had the habit while my children were still young of inventing and telling orally, sometimes of writing down, 'children's

stories' for their private amusement—according to the notions
I then had, and many still have, of what these should be like in style
and attitude."

57. Tolkien, *Hobbit*, 132.

58. "Had they followed the pass, their path would have led them down
a stream from the mountains . . . and to the entrance of the old
forest road. But Beorn had warned them that that way was now
often used by the goblins, while the forest-road itself, he had
heard, was overgrown and disused at the eastern end and led to
impassable marshes where the paths had long been lost" (*The Hobbit*,
117–8).

59. An ell is a measure of length, now little used, varying in different
countries. In England, it's equal to forty-five inches.

60. Tolkien, *Hobbit*, 125–6.

61. Ibid., 177–8.

62. Ibid., 186–7.

63. Tolkien, *Lord of the Rings*, 298.

64. Ibid., 391.

65. Ibid., 633.

66. Tolkien, *Hobbit*, 191.

67. Miller, *Blue Like Jazz*, 118.

68. Ibid., 125.

69. Tolkien, *Silmarillion*, 222.

70. Tolkien, *Hobbit*, 209.

71. Tennyson, *In Memoriam*, xcvi.

72. Rubie and Provost, *How to Tell a Story*, 61.

73. Peter wrote this letter to first-century believers in five different regions of Asia Minor, many of whom were being persecuted. He encouraged them to follow the example of Christ, who "entrusted Himself to Him who judges justly." The Greek word for "entrusted" is *paradidomi*, which literally means "to hand over."

74. Elliot, *Journals*, 174.

75. Tolkien, *Hobbit*, 237.

76. Solzhenitsyn, *Gulag Archipelago*, 75.

77. Pascal, *Pensées*, 110.

78. Marsh and Bamford, *Celtic Christianity*, 16–7.

79. Kelly, *The Best of Pogo*, 224.

80. Tolkien, *Letters*, no. 17, p. 24.

81. Ibid., no. 35, p. 42.

82. Tolkien, *Hobbit*, 50.

83. Tolkien, *Letters*, no. 339, p. 419. Unfortunately, this story was never completed.

84. Ibid., no. 213, p. 288.

85. Ibid., no. 93, p. 105.

86. Tolkien, *Hobbit*, 243.

87. See also 1 Kings 4:25; Zechariah 3:10.

88. Tolkien, *Lord of the Rings*, 1069.

89. Tolkien, *Unfinished Tales*, 343–44.

90. Tolkien, *Letters*, no. 191, p. 252.

91. Ibid., no. 192, p. 253.

92. Ibid., no. 328, p. 413.

93. Ibid., no. 191, p. 252.

94. Quoted as an epigraph to George MacDonald's *Phantastes: A Faerie Romance*, in MacDonald, *Phantastes and Lilith*, 14.

95. Tolkien, *Letters*, no. 203, p. 262.

96. Ibid., no. 262, p. 351.

97. Ibid., no. 135, p. 165.

98. Ibid., no. 66, p. 78.

99. Ibid.

100. Ibid., no. 203, p. 262.

101. Ibid., no. 163, p. 212.

102. Ibid., no. 109, p. 121.

103. Lewis, *Surprised by Joy*, 146.

104. C. S. Lewis, introduction to MacDonald, *Phantastes and Lilith*, 12.

Bibliography

Aelfric. *Aelfric's Lives of the Saints*. Edited by W. W. Skeat. London:
   Early English Text Society, 1881–1900.

Bonhoeffer, Dietrich. *The Cost of Discipleship*. New York: The
   Macmillan Company, 1959.

Bruner, Kurt, and Jim Ware. *Finding God in the Land of Narnia*. Carol
   Stream: Tyndale House, 2005.

——. *Finding God in The Lord of the Rings*. Carol Stream: Tyndale
   House, 2001.

Carpenter, Humphrey. *Tolkien: A Biography*. New York: Ballantine
   Books, 1977.

The Catechism of the Catholic Church. New York: Image/Doubleday,
   1995.

Clement. *The Epistle of Clement to James*. In *The Ante-Nicene Fathers*. Vol.
   8. Grand Rapids: Wm. B. Eerdmans Publishing Company, 1976.

Elliot, Jim. *The Journals of Jim Elliot*. Edited by Elisabeth Elliot. Old
   Tappan, New Jersey: Fleming H. Revell Company, 1978.

Grotta-Kurska, Daniel. *J. R. R. Tolkien: Architect of Middle-earth*.
   Philadelphia: Running Press, 1976.

Kelly, Walt. *The Best of Pogo*. Edited by Mrs. Walt Kelly and Bill
   Crouch, Jr. New York: Simon & Schuster / Fireside Books, 1982.

Kilby, Clyde S. *Tolkien and The Silmarillion*. Wheaton: Harold Shaw
   Publishers, 1976.

Lewis, C. S. "Sometimes Fairy Stories May Say Best What's to Be Said." In *Of Other Worlds*. Edited by Walter Hooper. New York: Harcourt, Brace & World, 1966.

———. *Surprised by Joy*. Glasgow: William Collins Sons & Co., 1955.

Livy. *The Early History of Rome*. New York: Penguin Classics, 1960.

Marsh, William Parker, and Christopher Bamford. *Celtic Christianity: Ecology and Holiness*. Hudson, NY: Lindisfarne Press, 1987.

MacDonald, George. *Phantastes and Lilith*. Grand Rapids: Wm. B. Eerdmans Publishing Company, 1964.

Miller, Donald. *Blue Like Jazz*. Nashville: Thomas Nelson Publishers, 2003.

Mills, David. "Take Me!" *Touchstone: A Journal of Mere Christianity*. August 9, 2003. http://www.touchstonemag.com/blogarchive/2003_08_03_editors.html

Otto, Rudolf. *The Idea of the Holy*. Oxford: Oxford University Press, 1923.

The Oxford Dictionary of Quotations. Oxford: Oxford University Press, 1941.

Pascal, Blaise, *Pensées*. Translated by A. J. Krailsheimer. New York: Penguin Classics, 1966.

Rubie, Peter, and Gary Provost. *How to Tell a Story: The Secrets of Writing Captivating Tales*. Cincinnati: Writer's Digest Books, 1998.

Solzhenitsyn, Aleksandr. *The Gulag Archipelago 1918–1956*. New York: HarperCollins, 2002.

BIBLIOGRAPHY

Tennyson, Alfred, Lord. *In Memoriam*. In *Idylls of the King and a Selection of Poems*. New York: Signet, 1961.

Tolkien, J. R. R. *The Hobbit*. Boston: Houghton Mifflin Company, 1977.

———. *The Letters of J. R. R. Tolkien*. Edited by Humphrey Carpenter. Boston: Houghton Mifflin Company, 1981.

———. *The Lord of the Rings*. Boston: Houghton Mifflin Company, 1983.

———. *The Silmarillion*. Boston: Houghton Mifflin Company, 1977.

———. "On Fairy-Stories." In *Tree and Leaf*. In *The Tolkien Reader*. Edited by Christopher Tolkien. New York: Ballantine Books, 1966.

———. "The Quest of Erebor." In *Unfinished Tales*. Edited by Christopher Tolkien. New York: Random House / Del Rey Books, 1980.

Tolstoy, Leo. *Christianity and Patriotism*. Honolulu: University Press of the Pacific, 2002.

Faith is an ongoing adventure, not simply a one-time choice. "The Road goes ever on and on," as Bilbo regularly reminded Frodo. Once we hear the knock on the door and step onto the Road, there's no turning back. Life will never be the same again.

Are you ready for the adventure?

⟡⟡

The perfect tool for the young adults in your life—read either alone or in group study.

FROM BEST-SELLING AUTHORS
KURT BRUNER AND JIM WARE . . .

FINDING GOD IN THE LORD OF THE RINGS
Uncover the deep connections between Earth and Middle-earth, and let yourself be newly inspired by this tale of hope, redemption, and faith against all odds.

FINDING GOD IN THE HOBBIT
Jim Ware reveals the latent themes of virtue, salvation, and God's sovereignty that underscore J. R. R. Tolkien's original fantasy of Middle-earth.

FINDING GOD IN THE LAND OF NARNIA
Discover the deep spiritual themes of redemption and grace found in the popular Chronicles of Narnia by C. S. Lewis.

Available Spring 2007!
FINDING GOD IN THE STORY OF AMAZING GRACE
Bruner and Ware explore God's hand at work in the true stories of William Wilberforce, John Newton, and the end of the British slave trade.

SaltRiver Books are a bit like saltwater: Buoyant. Sometimes stinging. A mixture of sweet and bitter, just like real life. Intelligent, thoughtful, and finely crafted—but not pretentious, condescending, or out of reach. They take on real life from a Christian perspective. Look for SaltRiver Books, an imprint of Tyndale House Publishers, everywhere Christian books are sold.

SALTRIVER®

Intelligent. Thought-provoking. Authentic.
www.saltriverbooks.com